From here
We Changed the World

AMAZING STORIES OF PILGRIMS AND REBELS
FROM NORTH NOTTINGHAMSHIRE
AND WEST LINCOLNSHIRE

Adrian Gray

Bookworm of Retford

Copies of this book are available from
Bookworm, The Retford Bookshop, 01777 869224
and from most high street and online bookshops

Overseas enquiries can be made to
sales@bookwormretford.co.uk

First published 2016
Bookworm of Retford
1 Spa Lane, Retford Notts. DN22 6EA
www.bookwormretford.co.uk

Printed by www.burgessdesignandprint.com, Retford.

ISBN 978-0992785734

TO JOHN, MARGARET AND RICHARD

'HE IS NOT THE GOD OF THE DEAD BUT OF THE LIVING.'

ABOUT THE AUTHOR

ADRIAN GRAY studied history at Cambridge and has written over twenty books. He has been a teacher, one of Her Majesty's Inspectors of Schools, and an international education consultant. He is historical adviser to the Pilgrims & Prophets and Bassetlaw Christian Heritage groups. He is an active member of the Retford Baptist church and lives with his family in North Nottinghamshire.

The Pilgrims and Prophets team are happy to accompany or organise group tours, or to talk to local and church groups, with profits from the talks and tours going back into their work. You can contact them through their website or on Facebook pages. Bassetlaw Christian Heritage organise special events and exhibitions in North Nottinghamshire.

http://pilgrimsandprophets.co.uk/

https://www.facebook.com/PilgrimsAndProphets

INTRODUCTION

WHAT IS SPECIAL ABOUT NORTH NOTTINGHAMSHIRE AND NORTH-WEST LINCOLNSHIRE?

Quite simply this: given that it is a small, rural area, it has had a huge impact on Christianity in England, America and worldwide.

A circle thirty miles in diameter, centred on a point midway between the market towns of Retford and Gainsborough, will encompass a rural area that has had an enormous global impact on Christianity. Pretty well every English-speaking nonconformist congregation in the world can trace its origins here and, if we include the south Nottinghamshire birthplace of the effective founder of the Church of England, Archbishop Thomas Cranmer, then we could say every English-speaking Protestant church – this from a handful of villages and market towns. To this we may add that a handful of people from the same area were the first to openly advocate full religious freedom – for all faiths - 400 years ago with profound influence on the American Constitution.

Saint Paulinus got the Victorian-style stained glass treatment and looks here very little like the description of him recorded by the Venerable Bede, who had not anticipated him clutching a model of York Minster. (Author's collection)

There were probably a few Christians here before the fourth century but Christianity was re-established in 627AD when Paulinus and Edwin – both future saints – baptised the people of Lindsey in the River Trent, most likely at Littleborough. Saint Edwin was later killed in battle against the pagan Mercians and – briefly – buried in Sherwood Forest near Edwinstowe. The kingdom of Lindsey was a client kingdom to Northumbria, which may explain why there were bishops of Lindsey from 678 up until about 1011.

From 700 until 1066 our region suffered much from war – partly between the Kingdoms of Mercia and Northumbria, but also because the Vikings used the Trent as a highway and Gainsborough as a camp. Viking hatred of Christianity is reflected in the legend of Saint Edmund 'slaying' Sweyn Forkbeard at Gainsborough.

The Normans created new counties, broadly using the Trent as a boundary, but with Axholme in Lincolnshire. They created a Lincoln diocese in 1072, which meant the county boundary also separated the Church provinces of York and Canterbury. They built churches and abbeys such as Worksop and Rufford – partly because of fear of divine judgement. Monasteries produced great medieval works like *The Cloud of Unknowing* or the *Tickhill Psalter*. Sometimes great religious leaders, such as Hugh of Avalon, Bishop of Lincoln, rose to the top. Although the power of the Roman Catholic Church was great, there were dissident voices: we should also mention Bishop Robert Grosseteste and John Wycliffe, the fourteenth century reformer, who held the living of Fillingham in Lincolnshire.

Saint Hugh is depicted in many stained glass windows, most of which provide a Victorian 'High Church' concept of him! (Author)

For 900 years the Pope remained the ultimate Church authority but from 1534 Henry VIII began the English Reformation – just as the first 'Protestants' in Worksop were being put under pressure. Henry chose, as his first Protestant Archbishop of Canterbury, Thomas Cranmer from south Nottinghamshire. At first the main impact in our region was the closure of monasteries such as Beauvale, Mattersey, Worksop and Axholme from which families like the Lassells, Wrays and Tyrwhitts benefited. Others suffered: the priors of Beauvale and Axholme argued against dissolution, refused to take the Oath of Supremacy and, having denied the authority of the King out of loyalty to the Pope, they were executed in May 1535 along with John Houghton, the previous Prior of Beauvale.

Abbeys like Welbeck and Rufford went more quietly but there were significant rebellions in east Lincolnshire and Yorkshire. The dissolution indirectly helped the growth of the Protestant faith because Protestant families, such as the Willoughbys, Manners, Husseys and St Pauls, gained former monastic lands and then appointed parish clergy with evangelical ('Bible-based') views.

The sacrifice of Protestant martyrs like Anne Askew and John Lassells was immortalised in early prints and their story told to generations through 'Foxe's Book of Martyrs.'

Thomas Cranmer had extensive Lincolnshire connections, whilst locals like George Lassells, of Sturton and Gateford, worked with Thomas Cromwell in dissolving monasteries.

Henry's Church revolution was cautious: there was change at the top, but theology changed little and a reaction soon set in. George's brother John Lassells, whose guardian had been Sir John Hercy of Grove, was an influential 'evangelical' within King Henry's court. Denounced by his enemies, he was burnt at the stake in 1546 for challenging the King's views on the nature of the bread and wine in the Mass. Alongside him was the remarkable Anne Askew, a Lincolnshire woman with Nottinghamshire connections, also burnt because of her beliefs. Anne was – illegally – tortured in the Tower of London to gain evidence against Queen Katherine Parr by her reactionary enemies. Parr had close associations with Gainsborough.

Askew, Lassells and Parr certainly knew another Lincolnshire noblewoman, Katherine Willoughby, who was a great supporter of progressive reformist clergy. She escaped with her life perhaps because she was very powerful and able to live abroad during Mary's reign when persecution increased. Local evangelical clergy who had married, like William Denman in Ordsall and Thomas Brumhedde of Rampton, also had problems in Mary's time; Denman was nephew to Sir John Hercy, Lassells' guardian.

Sir Thomas St Pol. (St Paul.) and his wife Faith Grantham dominate the centre of the extraordinary church at Snarford (Author)

When Elizabeth came to the throne, a few who could not accept the Protestant faith lost their places, notably Thomas Watson, Bishop of Lincoln. Many ritualistic items were removed from churches including holy water vats, 'paxes' and rood screens, although that at Coates survives to this day. However, more sermons being preached meant that more pews were installed. There was also an increase in the number of clergy, and they were better educated; this, in a way, sowed the problems for the future!

In the Trent valley a network of people wanted to reform the Church of England further. Lassells and Askew had been part of this. Trust and faith were built by families. Askew's sister Jane married into the St Paul family who, two generations later, were powerful advocates of reform from their base at Snarford. Her grandson Sir George St Paul married Frances Wray of Glentworth, whose mother had exemplary evangelical connections. Frances's sister Isabel and brother Sir William Wray were systematic patrons of reforming clergy, such as Richard Bernard of Worksop and associates of John Smyth, from 1590 to 1620. Around Retford, families like the Denmans, the Hercy family at Grove and Helwys family of Askham and Saundy, also used their influence to place 'godly' clergy into local churches. Ordsall, Marnham, Babworth, Headon and Scrooby saw a succession of clergy who wanted to continue the Reformation. James Brewster was the Puritan rector of Sutton-cum-Lound; his brother William Brewster controlled the curates at Scrooby and Bawtry in the 1590s, similarly appointing 'Puritans' as they now became called.

The Church's approach to these dissidents was often ambivalent. Grindal and Sandys, archbishops at York, and their Nottingham archdeacons like John Louth were sometimes tolerant, but when Whitgift became Archbishop of Canterbury in 1583, control gradually tightened. The new archdeacon of Nottingham, John King, was keen to support the archbishop. Whitgift tried to make the clergy subscribe to his Three Articles of which one, the full use of the Prayer Book, became a significant conflict. Catholics were also persecuted in this period and Lincolnshire's Richard Topcliffe was especially notorious for his torturing of them. For a time, Puritan clergy like Richard Clyfton survived with powerful local protection. From 1593 the law on non-attendance at church was tightened further and the concept of 'nonconformity' was reinforced.

What did the Puritans want? In some ways it is easier to define what they did not want. They disliked 'Popish' ritual: the wearing of surplices, signing with the cross at infant baptism, kneeling at communion, the rigid application of Prayer Book text. They wanted better teaching from the Bible, as Brewster was doing by repeating Clyfton's Babworth sermons in the church at Scrooby.

Although there were clusters of puritans in other areas such as Kent, they were especially strong in North Nottinghamshire and West Lindsey. Why? Past arguments that this was some sort of lawless 'frontier zone' have ignored the strength of local factors. We know significant members of the gentry used their wealth and status to place 'godly' men into parishes over decades; Katherine Willoughby set the pattern in the south and east of Lincolnshire and others used the 'advowson' and patronage systems similarly, such as the Wrays, Hercy and the Denmans.

They were so effective because for sixty years the connections between the puritan families of the two counties created an impressive network of knowledge and strategy. Around 1600 the Wrays and St Pauls were connected to almost every other significant puritan family within fifty miles, so were able to identify and place talented young men into key churches; David Marcombe has shown the same system around Retford with the Hercys and Denmans, who were connected by marriage to the Travers family – nationally significant puritans.

Another reason is that the parish system left some places neglected, with either a 'chapel of ease' or no place of worship at all, or with too little income to attract an incumbent. Bawtry and Austerfield were 'chapels' of Blyth; Bawtry and Scrooby did not become parish churches in their own right until the seventeenth century. Such places could be 'served' by a curate who might be 'godly.' Both counties had large numbers of parishes which yielded only a low income and were often neglected or served by pluralist vicars; gaps could be filled with Puritan curates.

Although it has been suggested that the 'frontier' between the Church provinces of York and Canterbury made our two counties 'border country', this theory does not fully explain what was happening. In one suggestion, men could 'hop across' the border, but few -- perhaps John Smyth - appear to have done this. Moreover, puritans like the Wrays worked in both counties. More influential was the tolerance of Church authorities: because of the greater threat from Catholics in the York diocese in particular. Persecution in Nottinghamshire increased after a change in the archdeacon of Nottingham, whilst men like Richard Bernard survived because the Archbishop of York wanted to keep him.

James I's 1604 Hampton Court Conference and its conservative results proved a bitter disappointment to the Puritans and was bound to be a problem in an area that by 1605 had produced some of the leading religious radicals in England. Richard Clyfton at Babworth was established as a great puritan preacher whilst two men from Sturton-le-Steeple, John Smyth and John Robinson, were becoming influential theologians. At Worksop, Richard Bernard was also a progressive reformer. In 1605-6 half a dozen local clergy were 'deprived' of their offices, most famously Richard Clyfton, although most continued unofficial preaching. There is a remarkable reference to Bernard, Smyth and Robert Southworth walking together near Worksop and discussing 'Separation', but after a meeting at Isabel Wray's Coventry house in 1606 only some decided to separate; probably Clyfton and Smyth did so around April 1607. Indeed according to John Cotton it was Smyth who had called for the meeting at Coventry, and who influenced Clyfton in deciding to separate; the importance of Smyth has perhaps been underplayed. Thomas Helwys and Hugh Bromhead (likely connected to 'Brumhedde' of Rampton) of Wheatley followed in about September 1607.

Clyfton, Robinson and Brewster formed their own 'Separatist' congregation at Scrooby Manor (although meetings in Scrooby long preceded this) – and Clyfton continued to appear in other local churches. John Smyth and his friend Thomas Helwys formed a congregation at Gainsborough, but Smyth may have been in Holland by the year's end. An attempt to get away via Boston ended with Brewster in gaol for a time but by 1608 almost all had gone to Holland via Immingham (Stallingborough), mainly paid for by Helwys. But we should not forget that the majority of the puritans stayed at home.

Tobie Matthew, the Archbishop of York from 1606-1628, pursued a policy of chasing down lay and clerical 'schismatics' whilst also making efforts to retain some within the Church. He emphasised his points in preaching at Bawtry in 1607.

The Pilgrim ships put in at Dartmouth after Southampton and before they ever got to Plymouth, but it is the latter that is famous as their point of departure. (Author's collection)

The Scrooby group settled in Leiden and in 1620 some sailed to America: the Mayflower Pilgrims included locals such as William Brewster (Scrooby), William Bradford (Austerfield), Katherine Carver (Sturton) and her husband John Carver (possibly Sturton); John Robinson, their leader, also from Sturton, stayed in the Netherlands.

Smyth and Helwys became Baptists in 1609 before Helwys returned to England in 1612 to start the English Baptist Church. Before he died that year, Smyth penned the first clear argument for removing the Christian life from government legal control whilst Helwys soon went further by writing the first full argument in favour of freedom of belief for ALL faiths – but was arrested and died in Newgate Prison by about 1616.

His ideas of tolerance were further developed by John Murton, a Baptist from Gainsborough, and then by Roger Williams, who married Mary the daughter of Richard Bernard and set up Providence, Rhode Island. When Williams returned to England in 1643-4 he wrote in defence of Murton's views.

All of these had also rejected the harsh Calvinistic beliefs of the Robinson congregation, which had transferred to New England, in favour of a more 'Arminian' outlook. At the time they remained in a small minority but over the succeeding centuries their views have gained ground.

The signing of the 'Mayflower Compact' was recorded in stained glass and installed at Austerfield 400 years after William Bradford's christening here. (Author)

The 'second wave' of pilgrims to New England included the Williamses, but also a significant group from east Lincolnshire. These included the famous John Cotton from Boston, but also Hanserd Knollys, much influenced by Gainsborough separatists, who later returned to England. The governor across the Atlantic in this controversial period was Sir Henry Vane, who returned to Lincolnshire and married another of the Wray family, but was ultimately executed by Charles II.

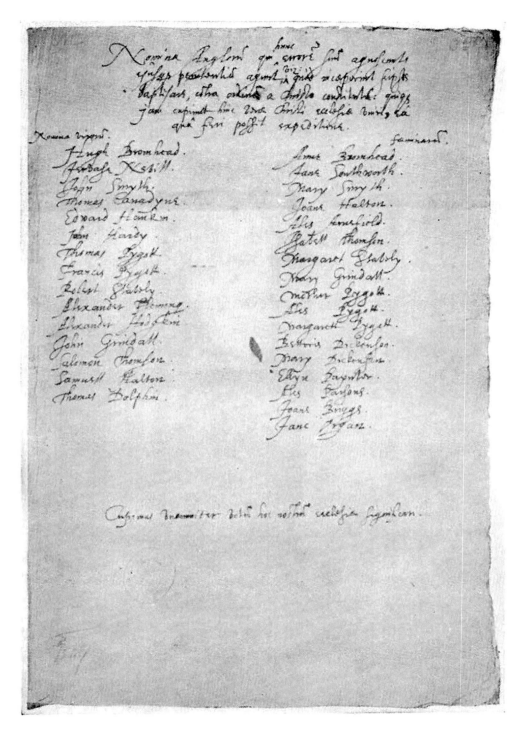

One of the last lists of Smyth's fellowship in the Netherlands including names of local interest such as the Bromheads.

Amongst nonconformists, Baptists started to become established by the late 1620s in Lincoln and Axholme and a few Congregationalist or Presbyterian congregations were also set up. The Quakers began in Mansfield in the 1640s, led by George Fox, with a markedly distinct theology of 'inner light'. An early convert was Elizabeth Hooton of Skegby; she became a famous Quaker missionary to America and the Caribbean. The first Quaker to die for his beliefs was a twenty year old from Retford, James Parnell, in 1656. Many Quakers were imprisoned in 1660 as the Restoration brought less tolerance, and Hooton went to prison often, although around Winteringham Quakers enjoyed some protection from Sir John Wray.

Puritans are often depicted in simple, often black, clothes but the memorials to Frances Wray show that not all of them had such restricted tastes. (Author's collection)

During the Civil War and the Protectorate, there were many changes to parish life. Clergy were driven out or replaced according to their views, so when Charles II reclaimed the throne in 1660 there was much to be 'managed'. In 1662 clergy who opposed the Restoration or infant baptism, such as Moses Mell at Kirton in Lindsey, were 'silenced' or removed. A new Book of Common Prayer in 1662 had to be accepted by all clergy, and this weeded out even more, with churchwardens supposedly keeping watch over their priest.

However, the Church of England had not consolidated its hold over people's lives – often for generations. When William Quipp was accused of preaching at Morton without permission in 1662, he justifiably retorted that the people had asked him as they had no vicar: there hadn't been one for decades. Other places were 'chapels of ease', getting irregular services; even many parish churches had only one weekly service and preaching was variable.

Between 1660 and 1690 the national stance on religious tolerance changed frequently. Charles II had promised religious tolerance, but after the 1661 Venner Rising gave Baptists a bad name the government sought to re-establish strict control of religion and conformity to their model of the Church of England through the Corporation Act, 1661, and the Act of Uniformity, 1662. From September 1661 worship was permitted only in authorised churches and chapels, or in private houses if only the people living there took part. The Quaker Act of 1662 banned five or more people from worshipping together and was later expanded to include all dissenters. Penalties were increased by the Conventicle Acts of 1664 and 1670, and although the Declaration of Indulgence, 1672, allowed some licences to be issued it was soon revoked. In Nottinghamshire, Justices Thoroton and Whalley launched their own anti-Quaker campaign in 1669, increasingly using informers who visited meetings and tried to prompt some into 'preaching.' It was not until the Toleration Act of 1689 that non-conformists began to enjoy some freedom of belief and worship, although Catholics did not benefit.

Lincolnshire men like Thomas Grantham played a significant role in strengthening the Baptists; by 1695 the Lincolnshire Association was well organised. By the early 1700s the Baptists were relatively strong in both counties, especially Lincolnshire; there were some Presbyterian congregations but Quakers were scattered and few. It can be argued that Quakers decided to 'quench the Spirit' by discipline, and in 1675 the Gainsborough congregation were already trying to stop 'sighing', 'groaning' or 'reverent singing.' John Whitehead complained in 1682 that the old generation who had seen the 'wonders of the Lord' were being replaced by another that had 'heard more, but seen and experienced less, both of the wiles of Satan and operation of God's power.'

The Baptists experienced some problems in the 1700s, with many churches declining until they benefited from the revival in the 1790s. A famous Baptist, Dan Taylor, was baptised at Gamston near Retford, and he had a significant impact on our region from 1764, especially after the New Connexion was established in 1770. Although Baptists often repudiated Methodists, the New Connexion shared Wesley's Arminian theology.

John Wesley produced a new awakening in the Church from the 1740s, preaching in the open air in his home town of Epworth and nationally. Wesley was an Arminian, but his friend and rival, George Whitefield, was a Calvinist; Whitefield seems to have had little impact in our region despite his significant reputation, though he may have visited Gainsborough in 1767, and the Countess of Huntingdon's Calvinist preachers established a short-lived foothold at Gainsborough and Morton. Wesley tried to stay within the Church of England but eventually the Methodist Church was set up from 1795.

Wesley was concerned with the Church's neglect of Communion, which was available only four times a year in many parishes. As Wesley himself noted after a visit to Haxey, the established Church's system allowed some men to hold multiple livings - pluralism; they then lived in luxury elsewhere off an income intended for ministering to the needs of the local people, who were left in the care of an impecunious curate, if at all. The same problem that Wesley found in the 1760s had been equally evident in the 1660s.

The two Wesley brothers are depicted in a memorial window at Epworth - something that not all Methodists at the time were totally approving of! (Author's collection)

The Church of England of course still had evangelical clergy of its own, such as Thomas Adam at Winteringham, who had his own personal experience of conversion from reading the same books that Wesley loved.

There was also William Bassett of Glentworth and later Blyton, but the Bishop of Lincoln, Pretyman Tomline, did his best to suppress any 'enthusiasm' to the extent that Wesley wrote to him in 1790, arguing that he was driving Methodists out of the Church.

The patronage system, which Tomline infamously exploited, made things worse. At Worksop, once a strongly Puritan church, the Duke of Newcastle refused to consider any candidate for the position who might be subject to 'enthusiasm.'

However, for many poorer livings there were not many candidates, or benefices became 'prey' to pluralists, who combined several and brought in a low-paid curate. Laneham and Rampton shared curate John Irvine, who took the services in place of the absentees; his income was so low that he tried to start a school to supplement it. When he lost the Rampton role he was reduced to 10 shillings a week in 1842 - the equivalent of about £30 today. But it was not all misery: John Bird, a curate who lived at Brigg in the late 1700s, held curacies in three parishes by keeping two horses - which he also used for hunting mid-week. In such places the church bell served a purpose –

it could be rung when the curate appeared on the horizon. Although 'Queen Anne's Bounty' made improvements from 1704 to the poorer livings, the best-connected clergy still picked off the richest.

Wesleyans were adept at filling the gaps, though prone to splits. By 1827, Lincolnshire had many Wesleyan chapels with two hundred and eleven compared to Nottinghamshire's seventy-seven; the Baptists had only thirty-one in Lincolnshire and seven in Nottinghamshire. However, the various Methodist groups made an excessive commitment to increasingly grand chapel-building and this weakened the organisation as a whole, including Primitive Methodists who went from camp meetings to imposing edifices in a few years.

The Primitive Methodist revival swept the countryside from 1817, stimulated by visits from the American revivalist Lorenzo Dow, to the 1850s, and in the 1870s influenced the early agricultural trade unions. It offered passionate revivalism with the chance for ordinary people to play a significant role; as the Wesleyans became more like the Church of England, the Primitives or 'Ranters' took their place, uniting, as R W Ambler has said, 'frontier-style revivalism with visions and prophetic insights'. In Gainsborough in 1818 their arrival was witnessed by the young Thomas Cooper (see Gainsborough). Old Methodists like Samuel Sharp of Messingham said that the revival fires were as in John Wesley's heyday and there was a 'great revival' in north Lincolnshire; the area north of Gainsborough was evangelised from 1819 to 1822 up to Swinefleet and Winterton, with thousands attending camp meetings.

The Primitive Methodists brought the style and fervour of the American campfire revivalists to the villages of the Trent Valley. (Author's collection)

William Braithwaite was the leader, who converted a farmer at East Stockwith after the man heard the preacher at prayer in a field: 'Thou must give me souls...Lord give me souls or I shall die'. And he did.

But Braithwaite was also fire and brimstone. It is told that when physically challenged by three men at Appleby, he prophesied none would die a natural death: one fell from a church tower, one was gored by a bull, and the other drowned in a dyke.

Like the Quakers before them, the Primitives used female preachers. They were looking for the ability to communicate with the folk the Wesleyans were leaving aside as they became more 'establishment'; John Bell of Sturton by Stow, a farm worker, became a circuit preacher only six months after his conversion. In their services and meetings they re-established the Pentecostal passion of the early Wesleyan days and were accordingly mocked by many. They built several chapels in Nottinghamshire in the 1820s and 1830s, converting a theatre in Retford in 1841. They continued to hold open-air camp meetings, such as on Spa Common in Retford. There was a notable revival around Scotter and Messingham in 1830: 'the country was baptised. Nearly every house was a house of prayer...'

Something of the same spirit was stirred up by James Caughey, an American Methodist evangelist, on his visits to Nottingham and Lincoln in 1846; however, he was often turned aside by Wesleyan Methodists and began to find the New Connexion more receptive. Caughey was followed by Walter and Phoebe Palmer with a style of evangelism that perhaps influenced Nottingham's William Booth, who enjoyed his first successes as a Methodist in Lincolnshire before going on to start the Salvation Army.

James Chalmers combined his missionary endeavours with a certain jingoistic approach which sits uncomfortably with some modern sensibilities, but ultimately he gave his life for the Gospel. (Author's collection)

Later missionaries criss-crossed the globe. John Hunt (Fiji) and James Chalmers (Papua New Guinea) had links with our area, and James Hudson Taylor's (China) mother was from Barton on Humber, the same town associated with Chad Varah who founded the Samaritans. Morris Gelsthorpe (1892-1968) spent years working in Africa and was eventually bishop of Sudan. Varah followed in the social mission tradition of William and Catherine Booth, who were influenced by poverty in Nottingham and went on to found the Salvation Army, which established a foothold in Gainsborough in 1886.

The Church of England made some necessary efforts to reform itself in the nineteenth century: in 1831 the Duke of Portland had been able to make legal provision to 'reserve' the living of Norton Cuckney for his infant grandson! Improvement was slow and in 1836 eighty Nottinghamshire clergy held two hundred and twenty-nine churches between them, with one holding seven livings. The Pluralities Act, 1838, attempted to control this ancient abuse; Bishop John Kaye of Lincoln was one of its architects along with James Monk, a son of the Harworth vicarage. However, patronage remained a challenge – three noblemen controlled twenty-seven parishes in Nottinghamshire and this barely changed during the 1800s.

The number of ordinands increased in the 1820s, so by mid-century most parishes had an educated, resident clergyman who would take two services on a Sunday. Perhaps the challenge of the Wesleyans could be seen in the greater frequency of Communion. The Nottinghamshire area of the diocese of York – the Archdeaconry of Nottingham – was moved to the diocese of Lincoln in 1835, and then the creation of the diocese of Southwell in 1884 completed a task which had first been considered by Henry VIII. In 1935 it returned to being in the Province of York. The general direction of all this was that the relevant bishop was able to play a much greater role in the life of the diocese and its clergy.

However, some of this energy was lost in the endless disputes over ritualism. The church at Owston Ferry – England's most Methodist place in 1851, where there was a bitter graveyard dispute – was rebuilt in ritualist style. Sometimes the locals revolted: in the 1840s in Nottinghamshire the wardens at Stokeham refused to wash the curate's surplice or provide a cup for the Eucharist, whilst nearby at East Drayton they refused to have bread and wine at all for two years; when the census was taken in 1851, only three people attended Stokeham. Thomas Mossman, vicar of Ranby, was an extreme ritualist who styled himself 'Bishop of Selby'.

A few understood the damage that could be done by petty disputes within and between denominations; when a new town graveyard was proposed at Gainsborough it was typically suggested that this be divided between Church of England and dissenters but the town's vicar said this was 'revealing to all the world our religious divisions and perpetuating them'.

The twentieth century saw much decline in overall church attendance, and the closure of many nonconformist chapels and rural churches. The 'redundant church' has become a feature of the landscape, and country vicars now have several churches to run without the financial benefits of their pluralist predecessors. From 2001, Anglicans and Methodists began working together more extensively in Lincolnshire to address the problem of serving rural communities. Yet it is not all downhill: a new denomination emerged in the Assemblies of God which grew up following the Pentecostal revival at the start of the century, and made Mattersey Hall their national base in 2012. They have churches in Retford, Gainsborough, Scunthorpe and elsewhere, whilst their training college is having a global impact. There have also been many new churches in towns and villages across the region, such as New Life and Hope churches in Gainsborough, and even in relatively small settlements like Scotter. Many of these are 'charismatic', with young congregations. Older congregations have rebuilt and rebranded, such as The Crossing in Worksop and The Well in Retford. The Groundlevel network, based in Lincoln, has had a wide influence. Duncan and Kate Smith have emerged from north Nottinghamshire as global leaders in the Catch the Fire network associated with the 'Toronto Blessing'; Kate went to school in Worksop whilst Duncan is the son of missionaries who worked in Nigeria – where he was born – and from Bawtry Hall.

From all of this, you as the reader can take this book in two ways. On one level it provides the history and stories of people and movements of common interest to all who live in or visit our area. For those who actively follow the faith, though, it is the family story of their brothers and sisters who share an understanding of what Jesus meant in referring to Exodus, 'I am the God of Abraham, the God of Isaac, and the God of Jacob,' and then adding 'He is not the God of the dead but of the living.'

Alkborough:

The village is famous for its turf maze, Julian's Bower. It has been claimed these commemorate St. Julian the Hospitaller, who set up a hostelry after accidentally killing his parents and was one night visited by a leper. As there were no spare beds, he offered his own to the leper, who then turned into an angel.

The nearby 'Countess Close' is associated with Frances, Countess of Warwick (see Snarford); in 1624 she used the manor to endow Magdalene College and further her Puritan ideals.

John Wesley preached here several times, although in June 1743 he found the people 'stupidly attentive'. In 1759 he arrived for church but found no service taking place, so preached in the churchyard to people who…

> '…had never heard this kind of preaching before. Many of them were in tears, and pressed after me into the house where we met the society. I could not but hope that some of these will press into the kingdom of heaven'.

In July 1770 he preached at 'Awkborough' simply on 'Christ crucified'.

Althorp:

The rector from 1648 to 1662 was Thomas Spademan. He was 'silenced' in 1662 but remained in the area despite the 'Five Mile Act'. In 1672 he became a Presbyterian minister in Boston. His son John went to Magdalene College, became for a time the incumbent at Swaton in Lincolnshire, and later pastored a Rotterdam church from 1680 after impressing with a trial sermon. In 1698 he went to London to pastor a Presbyterian church.

Matthew Horbery (1706-73) was a son of the vicar (also of Haxey), a theologian and noted by the famous actor Garrick as one of the best preachers he had ever heard.

Askham:

This was one of the manors held by the Helwys family in the late 1500s. Sir Gervase Helwys (1561-1615) was baptised here. He was a prominent local evangelical, who knew and supported John Smyth and the Gainsborough

Separatists, and he was uncle to Thomas Helwys, one of the most significant local church leaders. He unwisely became Lieutenant of the Tower of London; he was hung in 1615 following the poisoning of Sir Thomas Overbury. His death achieved great attention for he died repentant, expressing confidence in his salvation.

Thomas Helwys (c1575-c1615), a figure of great significance, was born into the same family, though his birthplace is uncertain – Askham is likely. Later, Thomas settled at Broxtowe near Nottingham and had many religious radical friends, such as Richard Bernard of Worksop and John Smyth, whose Gainsborough congregation he was connected with from about 1607. Smyth stayed with Helwys when he was ill in 1606 and Helwys possibly stayed at Saundby when attending the Gainsborough meetings. Smyth preached illegally at Helwys's church in Basford.

In 1607-8 Helwys was cited for not attending church or taking communion at Bilborough and Basford. Helwys helped to fund the move of the Separatists to the Netherlands, though his wife Joan, who was in prison in York at the time, never joined him there. In fact, Helwys had regularly been accused of living in fornication with Joan because of a dispute about their marriage. In Holland Helwys sided with Smyth in becoming a Baptist, but then split with Smyth when he decided it was his duty to return to England to effectively found the Baptist denomination in 1612 despite the risks.

Helwys is also of great importance for the section of his book, The Mystery of Iniquity, which argued that the State should have no control over religious faith – and advocated the same rights for all faiths. James I put him in prison and he was dead by 1616. Helwys is also important for arguing 'free will' rather than the prevailing Calvinist 'predestination', and for being the effective founder of the Baptist denomination in England.

There is a 'Thomas Helwys Baptist Church' near to where he lived at Broxtowe, but nothing in the village where he was most likely born.

Austerfield:

Christian history here dates from the Council of Austerfield in 702-3AD. There was a dispute between the northern Celtic Church, and the Rome-aligned southern Church over authority and the date of Easter in particular; Wilfrid, erstwhile bishop of York, had angered the Northumbrians in several ways and they had driven him out.

King Aldfrith of Northumbria arranged the meeting with the Archbishop of Canterbury presiding. Wilfrid had the support of the king of Mercia, but this was not enough to convince the Northumbrians.

The manor house at Austerfield dates back to the 16th Century and can therefore be confidently linked to William Bradford. (Author)

Wilfrid was forced to petition the Pope in Rome. Austerfield seems to have been chosen as it was convenient for the Mercians and the Northumbrians, who perhaps travelled by river.

William Bradford was born at Austerfield in 1590, orphaned, but was moderately wealthy. We have few sources to describe his youth but much later Cotton Mather said that at about the age of twelve he began to read Scripture and came under Clyfton's influence at Babworth; for this he received 'the wrath of his uncles and…the scoff of his neighbours.' He later joined the Scrooby congregation.

Bradford tried to reach Holland from Boston in 1607 and, after arriving in 1608, became an influential member of the community. He and his wife were on the Mayflower and in December 1620 he first saw running water in the Americas and, befitting his origin, used a northern word: 'We saw two becks of fresh water.' He is important as the dominant leadership figure for the first few decades of New England, and also an effective historian of its early development. There are suggestions that a lad on the Mayflower, William Butten, was from Austerfield; this is unproven but based on baptismal records for Austerfield in 1598 – perhaps rather old to be 'a youth' in 1620. A boy of a similar name was baptised in Worksop in 1605. William died on the voyage and is commemorated by a new housing estate.

- *A stone commemorating the Council of Austerfield.*

- *An interesting eleventh century church with a fascinating doorway.*

- *Some excellent stained glass celebrating the Pilgrims to which, famously, female figures had to be added.*

- *A manor house reputed to be Bradford's, just north of the church.*

The 11th Century church at Austerfield has an especially fine doorway, through which the infant William Bradford must have been carried for his baptism on 19 March 1589. (Author's collection)

A new housing estate in Austerfield has a fine image of the 'Mayflower' but there is no certainty about William Butten's origins. (Author)

WILLIAM BRADFORD
BAPTISED 1589
AT AUSTERFIELD

THE MAYFLOWER

COMPACT

S. Wilfred

S. Bertwald

The interesting, modern windows at Austerfield depict William Bradford and the signing of the 'Mayflower Compact.' There was a rather feeble attempt to include women and children as an afterthought! One of the windows in Austerfield church has a fine, but imaginary, image of William Bradford outside his 'home' church. He left the village at 18 - but appears older here! (Author)

Another window at Austerfield depicts the main protaganists in the famous Council - in rather unlikely modes of dress for the period! (Author)

Babworth:

This beautiful country church, set amidst trees at the end of an ancient 'sunken lane', is famous as the spiritual home of the Mayflower Pilgrims and their original pastor, Richard Clyfton.

The delightful painting of puritans on their way back from church at Babworth was the work of a prisoner at nearby Ranby Prison and reputedly included the likenesses of some of the inmates or staff. (Janie Berry)

Clyfton became rector in 1586, having spent a year at Marnham, but it was already a Puritan stronghold when held by Robert Lily. In 1591 Clyfton had a brush against authority when he was challenged for not wearing a surplice or using the sign of the cross at baptism. By the late 1590s Clyfton's preaching was attracting regulars from other parishes and in 1598 William Brewster was in trouble for 'gadding about'. These people were liable to a fine for non-attendance at their own parish church; those attending later included young William Bradford. Puritans like Clyfton hoped that the new king, James I, would move the Church of England in line with their views, but he did not. By 1604-5 the churchwardens were in trouble for not having a surplice or the latest Prayer Book and in 1605 Clyfton and several others were removed from their positions. In 1606 Clyfton, Robinson, Bernard, Smyth and Helwys all attended a 'summit meeting' of Puritans at Isabel Wray's house near Coventry, following which a minority of them chose to 'separate'. Clyfton perhaps followed Smyth in making this decision. Clyfton became pastor to the congregation at Scrooby and in 1606-8 was still active in churches at Sutton where William Brewster's brother was priest, whilst his own brother John was a Puritan churchwarden at Everton.

He went to the Netherlands in 1608, dying there in 1616. William Bradford wrote of him that 'Much good had he done, and converted many to God by his faithful and powerful ministry, and truth in preaching and catechising.' He was 'a grave and reverend preacher'.

George Turvin was Clyfton's replacement; the patron was Gervase Helwys (see Askham and Saundby) who had purchased the lordship. Turvin had started out as a Puritan but drifted into conformity. Anne Denman, a member of a prominent Puritan family in Retford and relative of Walter Travers - a famous Puritan at the time - then disrupted services in 1606 when she did not approve of the rituals.

Richard Clyfton's church at Babworth provides a wonderful example today of a quiet English churchyard - with no houses in sight! (Author)

Balby:

This was a centre of 'Seekers' in the 1640s and was visited by George Fox in 1651. As a result, Richard Farnworth was 'convinced' and became a fiery Quaker preacher. The Seekers became one of the first significant groups of Quakers in 1652. Fox was attacked here in 1652 and had to be rescued by an innkeeper. Margaret Killam was converted in 1651 and became a well-known travelling Quaker preacher from about 1653. Her husband spent nine years in York Castle and she was imprisoned in at least four towns. In 1660 Fox was back for the annual meeting, held in an orchard, and which he said 'thousands' attended. Troops were sent from York to stop the meeting, apparently riding overnight and arriving as Fox was standing on a stool to give his address. Fox managed to persuade the Captain to let them continue for an hour and to leave just a handful of troops, so the Captain went away and the remaining soldiers allowed the Friends to do more or less as they wished.

There were still regular meeting here in 1803 when Hannah Kilham, widow of Alexander (see Epworth) applied for membership after she had left the Methodists. Meetings were held at Doncaster, Thorne and Sheffield, where Hannah Kilham was based. Hannah later went to The Gambia and Sierra Leone as a missionary and translator. She was buried at sea off the coast of Liberia in 1832.

Barrow on Humber:

In 699 Ceadda (or Chad) became the Bishop of Mercia. Ceadda was a humble man and was reluctant to ride around his diocese on a horse 'to accomplish the work of the Gospel'; according to Bede, Archbishop Theodore told him to go by horse and lifted him bodily onto the beast. Ceadda was Bishop of Mercia and Lindsey, a task he approached with 'great holiness'. Wulfhere gave him land at 'Ad Baruae' (Barrow) for a monastery, but he set up his cathedral at Lichfield in Mercia. This is the first known Christian church outside of Lincoln in our region. When Caedda died in 672, his successor was the Abbot of Barrow, Wynfrith. However, within a few years Wynfrith fell out with Archbishop Theodore and was deposed. He returned to his monastery at Barrow, which was later presumed destroyed by Vikings.

In 1761 John Wesley arrived in Barrow, where the mob was in readiness, "but as more and more of the angry ones came within hearing, they lost all their fierceness". Barrow received fairly regular visits from Wesley. In 1764 he was "much pleased with their spirit and behaviour, and could not be sorry for the storm", which held him there overnight. In July, 1770, he recognised Barrow as a place for simplicity: Barrow folk he will not "take out of their depth, but explained and enforced these solemn words: 'It is appointed unto men once to die'". The first chapel was built there in 1780 (rebuilt 1868) and on 16th May, 1782, Wesley preached in the 'New House'.

In the late 1790s Thomas Edman had some problems with a female admirer, showing the perils of being a young Methodist circuit preacher:

> 'June 12th. Barrow. To-day as I was coming hither a delicate fair one met me upon the road and told me she wanted to speak to me. The poor creature looked as if she was fit to drop into the earth and said it was a matter of great importance. With much reluctance she got it out; her affections were placed upon me. So I told her she must place them on some other object. She hoped I would not expose her and wished to get over it as well as she could. I exhorted her to get an interest in Christ. She made no pretence to religion. She said she had heard preaching but never was profited thereby and where she had seen me I cannot tell I suppose in the chapel. But I don't see I can find who she is without exposing her tho' she told me her name, but I don't know whether I can remember it or not. O Lord have mercy upon me and give me grace that I may be enabled always to behave to all as becomes the Gospel. June 13th. Barrow. Last night as soon as I got into the pulpit I saw the young creature that met me upon the road and her face almost like a fire coal. I was somewhat affected at the sight knowing it was on my account. She hung down her head and seemed to be in a very dissatisfied state. I made enquiry but I could not find out who she is.'

Within days Edman was troubled by rumours about his 'relationship' and learnt to be wary of young women!

Barton on Humber:

By tradition, Chad (or Ceadda) was very active in Lindsey and the blow wells at Barton were reputed to have been used by him for baptisms - also the 'Shadwells' which were to the west, although the linking of this name to Chad is disputed. There may be no historical evidence, but they would have been an obvious venue for anyone planning some immersions.

The first church at Barton, St Peter's, is interesting as having been built in stone but using a methodology based on building with wood; it is one of the earliest Christian buildings in the country. Parts date from perhaps the ninth century with burials from the eighth. The town also had a 'Barley Bell' tradition, a type of curfew.

There is an apocryphal story that Wesley once preached in Barton, in the Market Place, and that the farmers passed a wagon-rope round the crowd, and with a horse at each end, gently drew preacher and people out of the Market Place. In fact in 1764 Wesley only passed through and used the ferry to Hull, but he did not enjoy the experience. He travelled with 'two such brutes as I have seldom seen. Their blasphemy, and stupid gross obscenity, were beyond all I ever heard'.

A correspondent to the Lindsey Observer provided some evidence of what actually happened:

'About 100 years since, the Rev. John Wesley, accompanied by a friend, came to preach at Ferriby. That both of them might be usefully occupied, this friend came over to try to get a hearing at Barton. Finding no place was open to him, he took his stand in the Market-place, near to where the Town's pump now is, and began to preach. My informant and a friend were among the hearers; when suddenly they were interrupted by a party (some of whom ought to have known better), who pelted the preacher with rotten eggs. When this barbarous sport had been carried on for a while, the leader of the mob, who, had he better understood the functions of his office, would have been exhorting the people to peace and good order, recommended them to pull him out of the town, which was carried into execution with a cart-rope. Now for the effect of all this. Two of the hearers followed the preacher to Ferriby, and enquired into the legality of these proceedings, and being informed that a place might be licensed for preaching, they, after due deliberation, went to Lincoln, and procured from the proper authority a license for a room in Old-Market Lane (now a cooper's shop). They were bitterly persecuted for a long time, but the more they were persecuted the more they increased. A large barn was then purchased (in 1788), and converted into a chapel. A second, third, and fourth followed.'

Perhaps John Wesley prophesied in June 1786 after a visit to the town, that 'Surely God will have a people in this place.' Amelia Hudson lived in Maltby Lane, Barton on Humber up to her marriage in 1831. Her father was the Methodist minister in charge of the Barton Circuit. Amelia's child, James Hudson Taylor, had a profound impact on missionary work, founded the China Inland Mission, and laid the foundations for what is likely to become the world's largest Christian nation with 90 million believers already; in global impact, he must now rank with Wesley.

Richard Watson (1781-1833) was born of humble origins in Barton (at the corner of Market Place and the Butchery) and converted to Methodism in

Amelia Hudson, mother of the great missionary James Hudson Taylor, was brought up in this house at Barton where her father was a Methodist minister. (Author's collection)

1794. After working as a preacher around Newark 1796-1801, he went on to become one of the most important Wesleyan theologians of the nineteenth century, a leading light of Wesleyan Mission, and an anti-slavery campaigner who famously wrote that 'Christianity will not snap the chains of the slave, but it will melt them'.

Chad Varah was born at Barton on Humber in 1911 and was the son of its vicar. He became a curate in St Giles, Lincoln, and then from 1949 to 2003 held various clerical posts in London. After a young woman committed suicide out of sexual ignorance, he became interested in sex education and then the problem of suicide, founding The Samaritans in 1953. The organisation spread internationally as 'The Befrienders' and even had a TV series made about it.

- *Visit the 'blow wells' and reflect on the possibility of early baptisms here.*

- *St Peter's Church and its ancient baptistery from a time when becoming a Christian really meant a step into Light out of pagan darkness.*

- *Take a walk around Maltby Lane (Hudson Taylor), the Market Place (Watson), the Old Vicarage on Beck Hill (Varah).*

Bawtry:

This town was certainly influenced by the Brewster family, as William's brother, James, was master of St Mary Magdalen Hospital from 1584. There were allegations that Brewster had abused his position and subverted the funds, leading to a lengthy legal battle against the Archbishop, and Brewster's being deprived of the position. The chapel was converted into a Masonic lodge in 1930.

Bawtry was not a parish in its own right but a 'chapel'; in 1605 Henry Gray, curate of Bawtry, was a Brewster associate and one of the Puritan priests who were 'silenced'. It is not surprising that when Archbishop Matthew visited Bawtry in September 1607 he preached an anti-separatist sermon, although Gray eventually 'conformed' and was licensed again as a preacher throughout the diocese in 1607.

John Wesley occasionally came this way but on one occasion found that those who were meant to have escorted him over the waterlogged ground to Epworth had gone. Fearing being swept away on a dark night, he was able to summon help at 'Idlestop' and an expert guide led him through the waters to safety.

Bawtry Hall, a former stately home and RAF headquarters, enjoyed many years as a Christian conference centre and the base for Christian charity or mission work by Action Partners until it closed; it was sold in 2014.

Belton (Axholme):

Belton had many nonconformists including some Baptists by 1640 and there were fifty-seven in 1669.

In 1742 Wesley preached here under a 'shady oak'. He was worried about a young man who 'saw the devil in every corner of the church'. On 18 April 1752 he preached and 'felt an uncommon degree of the presence of God, among an handful of poor, despised people'. When he was here in 1780 he was still talking of the 'dawn of a blessed work', but he was interrupted by 'My Lady's Preachers' -- the Countess of Huntingdon's men.

In 1786 three children from one family fell into a well during his preaching – and lay in it for half an hour. The children were brought to Wesley and feared dead, but his advice was to rub them with salt and to 'breathe strongly into their mouths'. Two revived, but the child who had been trapped beneath the bucket did not.

- *The site of early baptisms at Dipping House Farm can easily be identified as it is now a cattery.*

This farm near Belton in Axholme got the name 'Dipping House Farm' because baptisms took place in the river here - it hardly looks inviting! (Author)

Beauvale:

We include Beauvale because of its close links with the Mayflower Pilgrims. The Carthusian priory here was founded in 1343. It has been suggested that the *Cloud of Unknowing* was written by a monk of Beauvale. The dialect of Middle English used in *Cloud* suggests origins in the north-east Midlands. Other spiritual works are also likely to have come from Beauvale, such as *Speculum Vitae Humanae* in about 1390.

In 1535 the prior, Robert Lawrence, and three others went to see Thomas Cromwell to argue against dissolution. Having refused to take the Oath of Supremacy and thereby having denied the authority of the King, they were executed 4 May 1535 at Tyburn. Also executed was John Houghton, the previous prior of Beauvale, although he only held that post for around six months, and Augustine Webster of Axholme. Tradition relates that when Houghton was about to be quartered, and as the executioner tore open his chest to remove his heart, he prayed, 'O Jesu, what wouldst thou do with my heart?'. A painting by Francisco Zurbarán depicts Lawrence with his heart in his hand and a noose around his neck. Lawrence was beatified in 1886 and canonised in 1970; Webster and Houghton were also made saints.

William Trafford was sent to London from Beauvale in 1535 for refusing to accept the supremacy of the King and arrived a few days after Lawrence's execution. Having eventually 'conformed', he was made prior of the London Charterhouse in Houghton's place. By the time commissioners arrived to close Beauvale, the prior was all packed up and ready to leave. One of the last monks, the Sacrist Dugmer, claimed to have had a vision of Mary and the infant Jesus playing in the garden at Beauvale.

The Priory and its lands were awarded to Sir William Hussey, a Lincolnshire landowner. Hussey's daughter Neile married Richard Disney, of Norton Disney in Lincolnshire, by which the Disneys came to hold Beauvale. Disney's second wife was Jane Askew, sister of the famous Protestant martyr Anne, from a family who held lands both at Stallingborough in Lincolnshire and near to Beauvale at Nuthall. This established Beauvale and its parish church at Greasley as a Protestant enclave, which reached its peak when the White family from Sturton le Steeple arrived there; as we shall see, Bridget White married John Robinson, the famous Puritan leader, at Greasley in 1603/4. The mother of the Whites knew one of the Disney family, which may explain their move, although Charles White seems to have been involved in coalmining. Later Bridget, two sisters and a brother went to the Netherlands where one – Katherine – married John Carver and sailed on the Mayflower.

- *Little remains of the Priory but it is a wonderful setting with an on-site teashop. The isolation today perhaps explains its attraction for Puritan conclaves.*

The Priory at Beauvale rests now in a tranquil setting but has seen many significant events and people during its history. (Author)

Blyth:

The church is remarkable for the recent uncovering of its extraordinary fifteenth century 'doom painting', which is a powerful demonstration of how 'Christianity' was taught to the illiterate before the Reformation. There has been much debate over whether Francis Cooke, a passenger on the Mayflower, came from Blyth.

Blyth had a Quaker congregation meeting at John Seaton's house, but they were persecuted by the magistrates for holding illegal meetings. Seaton, who was the village carrier, lost all his household goods, his animals and building materials. Seaton was then fined £26 by Justice Thoroton for attending a meeting when he was in fact sixty miles away, and then this was overturned by a jury on appeal. The Justice was so angry he threatened to hang all the jury and told them they were worse than highwaymen. Ordinary people were unhappy about this persecution of 'godly' folk, and even the constable of Blyth had to be fined for refusing to collect the money owed. When Seaton died in 1700 he left money to fund two cottages for poor widows adjacent to the Quaker chapel at the corner of Oldcotes Road that had been built once their worship became legal. They were rebuilt in the 1760s whilst the Quaker chapel was taken over by the Primitive Methodists.

Blyton:

Wharton[1] was home to a branch of the Wray family; Sir William Wray (1555-1617) was an important supporter of John Smyth, who believed him to be the 'principal patron of godly religion in Lincolnshire'. Smyth dedicated his first book to Wray in 1603. Wray was brother to Isabel and Frances (see Glentworth/Snarford for this family).

Sir William appointed Thomas Rainbow as his vicar at Blyton. His child Edward (1608-84) had Edward Wray of Rycot as godfather. Frances Wray must have known Edward as the grandson of David Allen, a nonconformist supported by her first husband, and nominated him for a Wray scholarship to Magdalene College Cambridge – these were first created by her father, the Chief Justice. By 1630 Rainbow was master of the school at Kirton in Lindsey, returning to Magdalene and becoming its Master in 1642. He became Bishop of Carlisle in 1664, where his condemnation of immoral living made him enemies who blocked him from becoming Bishop of Lincoln. He seems to have moved away from Puritanism and died as 'an orthodox but moderate Anglican, sympathetic to nonconformists'.

---

[1] One mile south of Blyton, now a 'lost' settlement

William's son Sir John (c1586-1655) was described by Bernard as 'of more than ordinarie zeale for holiness and religion'. Although from a strong Protestant family, the family history sneeringly credits European travel for developing this in him: 'whither he travelled I know not, but he returned with a strong hatred of Papists and a love of hearing his own voice'. He supported more Puritan clergy through patronage, including Thomas Coleman who held the living at Blyton from 1623 until 1646, and was imprisoned for eight months for his opposition to the King. Wray went to gaol for refusing to pay the 'forced loan' to Charles I, even though his father-in-law offered to pay it for him. He was released in 1628 and then re-elected as MP for Lincolnshire. In 1630 he sided with the Axholme commoners against the King's drainage works. In Parliament, he was a critic of Ship Money.

He was active in organising Lincolnshire against the King but retired from politics in 1646, being buried at Glentworth in 1655. Wray left a memorial to his children in Blyton church.

Thomas Coleman left for London during the early 1640s, where he became a vocal critic of bishops and cathedral staff. He preached to the House of Commons in 1645 but was also known for his Hebrew scholarship and 'Erastian' views on the disciplining of non-believers during the Westminster Assembly of Divines in 1643, which discussed the future of the Church of England.

His face you see, but not his noble mind
That like his fame was great and unconfin'd;
Yet humble too, and honors would prevent:
But's virtues built the greatest monument,
Which all devouring time cannot deface,
Till the world wants both gratitude and grace.

Edward Rainbow built a successful career in the Church of England but seems to have never lost sight of his puritan origins in Blyton. (Author's collection)

Burnham (Axholme):

John Wesley preached here in 1742 and must have passed through many times. He first preached in the midst of the Epworth battle with Romley, as people were coming to hear him from Burnham believing they had to forsake their parish church.

He would therefore have probably been aware of its legendary 'holy well', which can still be traced by walking up the lane running east from the main road. This was regarded as having curative powers, especially at the Feast of Ascension, and was still frequented into the last century – there was even a pilgrimage to it. It is a good example of how science, paganism and Christianity could become muddled together in remote communities.

Clarborough:

Was this a 'Pilgrim Centre'? In 1623 in America William Bradford married Alice Southworth, widow of Edward Southworth; the possible link to the Southworths of Clarborough has been much debated. Jane Southworth was amongst those who left from Gainsborough for Holland; Thomas and Edward were also there – but where from? Jeremy Bangs, an international authority, suggests that the Thomas who was in Leiden in 1613 was the one of 'Welham in Clarborough' named in a Peck will of 1602.

Clarborough Vicarage looks serene in this late 19th Century picture, but vicars like Joshua Brooks appear to have had turbulent lives.

We also know, of course, that Robert Southworth – perhaps a different family branch – was closely associated with the Brewsters, and that there was an Edward in Clarborough in 1614-5. There was also a dissenting congregation meeting here in 1611 and a tendency to Puritan clerics, such as Nicholas Watkins who promised to conform; when Anne Peck had fled to the Netherlands, she left £7 with Watkins.

Joshua Brooks, vicar in the 1820s, was responsible for building St Saviour's Church, which, though physically in East Retford town, was geographically in Clarborough parish; he was a writer, and interested in prophecy. Clarborough was one of the first parishes where the right to nominate the next vicar was purchased by the Simeon Trust in the 1830s. This was a way of getting evangelicals into churches and followed the pattern used by the Wray sisters two hundred years before. One of the first appointments made was Rev Charles Hodge who, having entered the legal profession, turned instead to the Church. After being curate at Sturton and holding the living at Scofton, the Trustees appointed him to Clarborough – and made him resign Scofton. Hodge and his wife had ten children, after which she more or less ran away to New Zealand. Having briefly returned, she then put pressure on her husband and family to go back with her, and Hodge got a two-year absence agreed. At the end of this period he did not return, so legal steps were taken to compel him – which proved fatal.

Having left family behind, on 27 October 1859 he was lost in the wreck of the *Royal George* off Anglesey with about four hundred and fifty others. Brooks preached the funeral sermon at St Saviour's, referring to Hodge's undoubted 'infirmities and defects'. Hodge had lost money in New Zealand trying to set up his children, had had to borrow enough to come home, then was robbed even of this; Brooks still found time to allude to 'far darker' trials that were awaiting him on his return. Remarkably, parts of Hodge's diary were found after the wreck and published.

In 1854 George Fletcher, born here, was giving sermons in the Methodist chapel at Finsbury in London 'in his 108th year.' Fletcher attracted widespread publicity. He liked to tell stories of his military career, including being at the battle of Bunker Hill. Fletcher may well have seemed a paragon of Methodist virtue, for he claimed to have followed its disciplines since a child. The publicity attracted attention, and his story fell apart. The vicar of Clarborough reported that he had been christened in 1764, not 1747, so he would have been at Bunker Hill aged 11. In fact it seems he joined the army, deserted, and then re-joined, falsifying his age and record along the way to improve his pension; once he had added twelve years, it stuck to him. Even so, preaching twice on a Sunday at ninety or more was still impressive!

Clayworth:

A fascinating church, but a detail often missed is the brass of John Tonstall, rector from 1606 to 1630. A predecessor, George Monsonne, was 'deprived' under Mary I for being married, but was appointed to Orby in Lincolnshire a few years later, once Protestantism had returned; it's a good example of the uncertainties of the time.

This village was the home of the celebrated preacher, John Cromwell. He went to Magdalen, the Puritan college in Cambridge and was ordained and made rector at Clayworth in 1657, apparently because of the favour of his namesake Oliver. He lost this position in 1662 as it was argued he had been given it without right, and was briefly imprisoned at Newark in 1663 after the 'Yorkshire Plot', although the Duke of Newcastle tried to intercede on his behalf. One of those who 'prosecuted (him) violently' was Sir William Hickman. In Norwich he was sneered at by Anglican clergy during a dinner with the Bishop, who told his graceless colleagues that 'he has more solid divinity in his little finger than all of you have in your bodies'.

MONVMENTV ÆRE PERENNIVS

ortui immortalem memo

The brass of John Tonstall in Clayworth church - a strong image of a clergyman from the turbulent early 1600s.(Author)

William Sampson, born in South Leverton and with a Puritan mother from Treswell, was rector from 1672 to 1702, though not always here. However, his Rector's Book is one of the best historical sources of village life from the period. In 1694 he was elected Master of Pembroke College but refused. His brother Henry was ejected from his own living in 1660 and became a nonconformist and a doctor; his research on Puritan history influenced later historians. He died at Clayworth in 1700, being buried at his brother's church. In 1707 eminent church historian John Inett became rector, installing his sons as curates.

John Wesley must have first preached here in 1751 (possibly in May), as on 19 April 1752 he wrote that 'a year ago, the mob carried all before them. But an honest Justice quelled them at once, so that they are now glad to be quiet, and mind their own business'; again in 1755 and in 1757 when 'all were moved' but one man, Michael Fenwick, who famously fell asleep under a hayrick. However, there may be more to this story than at first seems evident; Fenwick was a young man who travelled much with Wesley but has been said to have been eccentric, 'with a weak head...but a good heart'. There is an apocryphal story that Fenwick complained to Wesley that he never got a mention in his Journal, so Wesley put him in; if so, it is a rare example of Wesley humour! In 1761 Wesley tried to reconcile two brothers who were arguing about an inheritance, to no avail.

The church is now famous for the Traquair Murals.

Clifton, North:

It is probable that John Smyth, the Separatist, was here as a schoolmaster and preacher in the years 1603-4; the village had a Puritan priest, John Nayler, around this time. In 1604 the churchwardens complained that both their priest and master were 'painfull preachers'.

Charles Kingsley, father of the author of The Water Babies, was vicar here from 1820 to 1832 and may have briefly been curate before that. His son, the famous author, was born in 1819 but must have spent only a limited time here as he was away at school. Kingsley senior combined North Clifton with being rector of Barnack near Stamford, the latter being a massively well-paid job, so Clifton was mainly left to a curate. The stipend at Barnack --£1200 – would have been worth about £800,000 a year in 2015 prices! Kingsley moved to Chelsea in London in 1836 and, identified as an evangelical, became involved with the London City Mission.

The younger Charles also entered the clergy. He was much affected by the suffering of the poor in London during the 1840s, and witnessed much of the Chartist activity with which Thomas Cooper (see Gainsborough) was connected. Kingsley became a Christian Socialist, though he was not a revolutionary as such. His novel Alton Locke, published in 1850, was about a poet-tailor who became a Chartist and eventually a Christian; if this sounds much like Cooper it was, because they had become friends, though Cooper was to reject and then rediscover his Faith. Correspondence from 1850 shows Kingsley just as concerned to reclaim Cooper for Christ as he was to espouse the benefits of the co-operative movement. Kingsley also became interested in sanitation, which brought Prince Albert's attention.

Kingsley saw a new concern in the rise of Catholicism in the mid-1800s, influencing his very popular novel Westward Ho! His academic and church career brought him to be Dean of Westminster Abbey. Mainly a writer for adults, he is, like Tolkien and Lewis, best known for a book he wrote for children – *The Water Babies* – published in 1862, although even here he was making adult points about social justice, fashion, and Darwin. Kingsley's time in the East Midlands can best be seen in the fenland aspects of his novel *Hereward the Wake*. It is an amusing coincidence that while the infant future author perhaps was spending a brief time at North Clifton, directly across the river at Fledborough was 'Mrs Markham', working on her children's history of England.

Coates by Stow:

This has always been a tiny village. In 1086 it had a population of six, rising to thirteen in about 1400. We have included it here as it is a great example of the problems the Church faced in serving a huge, rural area – and a remarkable survival of old styles. Coates has the only fifteenth century rood screen in Lincolnshire. The screen, in simple Early English style, has been sensitively restored. In the gallery above the rood screen is a painted figure of the Virgin Mary, just visible against the wood panelling.

It was reported in 1721 that a curate had served Coates for fifty years on payment of £13 a year – the equivalent of about £1200. The church was barely used, and there is a famous story of a drunken farmer who lost his horse, only for it to be found starved to death in the church. Look out for its teeth mark on the pews.

- *A fascinating, atmospheric gem where, somehow, regular worship has been sustained.*

The interior of Coates' farmyard church is one of the best preserved 'pre-Reformation' church interiors in the region, despite damage from a horse's teeth! (Author)

Collingham:

Brian Barton, the rebellious rector of South Collingham, had thirty-two years of court appearances up to his death in 1626 and was linked to the cases of many lay people – for example those cited for attending the wrong church or not having a child christened. The result was that the local population was 'disturbed' and that Barton was running 'in effect a Separatist congregation'. After his death, several were excommunicated. Vincent Alsop, born in South Collingham in 1630, was one of the 'silenced' ministers under Charles II and was thought to have been imprisoned for six months after he prayed for a sick person in Northamptonshire; he became a very influential Presbyterian. In contrast, in 1650 George Groom was found to be 'a drunkard and a swearer'.

Collingham was a successful Baptist fellowship founded in about 1660 under the leadership of William and Mary Hart, who licensed their house in 1672, with up to ninety members. This survived for a long period, and benefited from the Newark Revival of 1841, which was led by the Baptist evangelist, Thomas Pulford. Later it was a Calvinistic church and supported a 'mission' church in Sutton on Trent. William Hart (d 1699) left money to start one of the few Baptists schools ever known; it survived into the early 1900s. In 1672 Hart would have linked up with other Baptist licences at Sutton, Norwell, Muskham and Carlton; this was an important Baptist area. Despite this, the Baptist chapel in Collingham is now a house.

Cromwell:

The rector in the Protectorate period was Joseph Truman. In a short biography of Joseph we are told that his 'godly' father Richard had challenged villagers' use of a maypole on the Sabbath, the villagers getting their defence from Charles I's *Book of Sports*; Richard responded that God's law trumped the King's, whereupon the villagers complained to a Justice. The Earl of Chesterfield was keen on prosecuting but his son supported Truman. Truman lost £1500 on the legal case, but said that God so blessed him that he made up all the money, whereas those that had accused him ended their days in poverty and unhappiness. Richard Truman was clearly a man of some wealth and land.

Joseph was born in Gedling, attended Clare College and was briefly vicar of Ruddington, though he was far from a traditional Church of England clergyman. Following the Act of Uniformity in 1662, Truman, according to Calamy, refused to read all parts of the Book of Common Prayer because there were "lies in it"; he gave as an example the repeated use of the collect for Christmas Day, whose reference to 'born this day' could not be true of all days it was scheduled for! Calamy said the collect was amended in consequence, but it had actually been altered by a conference at the Savoy in 1661. After Cromwell he went to live in Mansfield and still attended the parish church, although he was frequently in trouble for religious offences, and even managed to get off a charge of outlawry by skilled argument. In the 1670s he took up writing and his works were republished into the twentieth century.

Cromwell is also a good example of the patronage system not working out as expected. The Duke of Newcastle appointed Rev Charles Fynes-Clinton in 1828, presumably on the basis of his ancestry, and then was shocked to find he'd appointed an evangelical. He did not make the same mistake in Worksop in 1847.

Crowle:

Like other Axholme parishes, Crowle has a long nonconformist tradition and had a large Congregational chapel, a Baptist chapel (claiming an origin to 1599, much disputed) and both Methodist and Primitive Methodist chapels.

During the 1860s a story was widely circulated that a Baptist church existed in Crowle as early as 1599 and was instrumental in converting John Smyth, the Baptist pioneer, to being a Baptist. A book published at that time reported that old documents had been traced to the possession of Rev Smith Watson at Butterwick in 1866, which recorded the story in detail. However, the documents held by Watson were then reported to have been lost after he died, but the deacons of Crowle Baptist Church verified that they had seen them.

This all happened close to the time when the Crowle church was being rebuilt and in 1879, and a plaque was put up on the outside to say it was the oldest Baptist church in England. It all seems very unlikely; Smyth attended the Coventry conference in 1606 to discuss separation from the Church of England but somehow this part of the story was not recorded by any of the participants. The Baptist Quarterly accepted many years ago that the Crowle minister Jabez Stutterd had been 'the innocent victim of forged records', but it still resurfaces as 'true'. There was, though, certainly a Baptist community in Epworth and Crowle by the mid-1600s.

There was an outdoor baptism in the river at Crowle in 1855, which attracted 1500 spectators; these events were a great evangelistic opportunity. Despite this, the church was struggling by the later 1800s and the Baptist congregations at Crowle, Epworth and Butterwick were united under one minister. However, the church closed in July 2010.

This town was also a centre of Quakerism.

Robert Durant was a clergyman, perhaps a curate, here, and 'a sweet mixture of humility and courteousness'. Nonetheless, he was ejected for non-conformity both from here and from Risby in 1662. For a time he lived at Reedness and preached there privately. After a time in York Castle he became a nonconformist in Sheffield where he introduced the practice of a monthly fast for the congregation. He was such a success there that when he died even the town's vicar, who might have been expected to be an opponent, expressed regret.

John Ashbourn (1607-1661) started as a Puritan and married into a significant Ipswich family; he was Puritan enough to be given the vicarage at Glentworth, but later became more conformist; he was killed by his insane brother-in-law. Solomon Ashbourn (1644-1711), born at Burton upon Stather, was the long-serving vicar of Crowle from 1669 to 1715. It was clearly not a task he enjoyed; when he died his tombstone recorded that he 'solemnly bequeathed the following verses to his parishioners":

'Ye stiff-necked and uncircumcised in heart and ears, ye do always resist the Holy Ghost. As your fathers did, so do ye. (Acts 7.51)'

'I have laboured in vain, I have spent my strength for nought, and in vain. Yet surely my judgement is with the Lord, and my work with my God.' (Isaiah 49.4')

The sprawling vicarage at Crowle was partly built by Samuel Ashbourne, a clergyman little approeciated by his own parishioners. (Author)

It's been claimed that the old vicarage opposite the church was built by Rev Ashbourn in 1701. Perhaps we should not be too sympathetic: Ashbourn pursued Quaker Thomas Winder for a £2 debt, which resulted in him being imprisoned in Lincoln Castle 1705-9.

This tombstone was sufficiently infamous for John Wesley to seek it out. After a good search he found it in the church but had to clean out the dirt to read its lettering.

Wesley preached here at least seven times. A local Justice, George Stovin, showed himself a supporter by dismissing Methodist preachers brought up on trivial charges in 1742. When he came in 1748 Wesley preached from inside the Justice's garden – which gave protection from 'so wild a congregation as I had not lately seen.' Such was progress in the town by 1779 that Wesley went out to find the infamous slab of stone and was able to reflect when he found it:

> 'But that generation, which was abandoned to all wickedness, is gone: so are most of their children. And there is reason to hope, that the curse entailed on them and their children is gone also. For there is now a more lovely work of God here, than in many of the neighbouring places'.

In 1780 Wesley preached to a good congregation. He reflected that people had said in the past, 'Can any good come out of Crowle?' but 'God's thoughts were not as our thoughts. There is now such a work of God in this, as in few places round about it'.

Wesley's friend was probably George Stovin (1696-1780) the antiquary, so we can assume he preached at Tetley Hall, Stovin's house. Near here is an old stone font, which reputedly was brought from the vandalised church at Sandtoft, perhaps by Stovin.

In 1861 the American Methodist evangelists Walter and Phoebe Palmer came and stayed with Rev Robert Brush. A large tent was used for meetings and, Phoebe wrote, 'powerfully has the convincing, converting and sanctifying Spirit been abroad in all our assemblies.'

- *The Ashbourn memorial is supposedly in the chancel, but perhaps covered by Victorian choir stalls as we could not find it!*

- *Ashbourn's imposing if rambling old vicarage is opposite the church.*

- *Tetley Hall and the font although there is currently no public access.*

Cuckney:

King Edwin, the Christian king of Northumbria, was threatened by an alliance of Mercian and Welsh, all with pagan faiths. On 12 October 633 Edwin was defeated and killed in the Battle at 'Hæthfelth', normally referred to as Hatfield Chase. For long this was assumed to have been at Hatfield near Doncaster, but more recently there have been claims that this event was at a clearing in the forest – 'Hatfield' – near Cuckney in Nottinghamshire. The contention that the whole district was called Hatfield adds more substance to this view. This claim is perhaps supported by the 1951 discovery of communal graves containing two hundred bodies, laid with their feet to the east, and the naming of 'Edwinstowe', meaning the sanctuary or burial place of Edwin – and much closer to Cuckney than Doncaster.

In 1638 the Duke of Newcastle was rumoured to be an atheist, fuelled by his Christmas masque lampooning Cuckney's Puritan clergyman, Francis Stevenson. William Otter (1768-1840), Bishop of Chichester, was born here; he also worked with Malthus on his famous population research.

Edwinstowe:

Legends relate that Edwin's body was brought to Edwinstowe after the battle of Hatfield Heath in 633; this may have been at nearby Cuckney and some historians take the view that Edwin's body was buried at Edwinstowe whilst his head was taken to York. It was written that the monk Trimma was told in a vision to collect the body and take it to Streanaeshalch (Whitby) which became a place of pilgrimage. Trimma lived on at the burial site in Sherwood and often saw the spirits of four of the slain, it was said, and who were 'certainly baptised persons who came in splendour to visit their bodies'.

This image of the very simple Primitive Methodist chapel at Edwinstowe was taken in 1938, but in some areas the denomination invested large sums in grandiose buildings. (Nottinghamshire County Council, Picture the Past)

The site of the chapel was identified in 1911 by the Vicar of Edwinstowe and W Stevenson, after which a cairn of some of the original building blocks was put up on the instructions of the Duke of Portland and surmounted by a metal cross. The earliest record of this is from 1201 when King John paid the hermit of Clipstone a stipend for his services, and payments are recorded to 1548. The chapel is shown on maps of 1610 and 1630, but little is known of whether it really marked Edwin's resting place. Of course Edwinstowe church is famously where Robin Hood married Maid Marian…which is even less likely!

John Featley, rector here in the 1660s, was the first 'preacher of the Gospel' on the island of St Kitts in 1626.

The legendary site of the the old Edwinstowe hermitage was rediscovered and an iron cross erected: does this mark where King Edwin was first buried? (Author)

Epworth:

Epworth was the birthplace of two significant Puritans: Richard Bernard (see Worksop) and Thomas Granger (c1578-1627). Granger was made vicar of Butterwick in 1606 and was a prolific author 1616-21; he is interesting in being a Calvinist who also favoured separation of the godly, but cautious to keep a safe place in the Church of England.

Epworth is, of course, most famous for the Wesleys, and it is the place of which John Wesley wrote in 1784 that 'I still love beyond most places in the world'. In 1600 the Isle of Axholme was indeed pretty well an island, surrounded by the marshes known as 'Carrs'. King Charles decided he could make money by using Dutch engineers to drain these for farmland, but this angered local people as they provided food and summer grazing. This contributed to the strong anti-Royalist feelings that ensnared the rector Samuel Wesley, with serious riots in the 1650s and in 1694 just before his arrival in 1695.

Riots at Epworth in 1650-1 were blamed on the Quakers, who were strong here. Richard Farnworth led meetings at Axholme where 'much fier kindled' and he wrote to Fox about events at Haxey which 'shaketh kingdoms and turns the world upside down'.

Quakers faced legal problems after the Restoration. In 1664 three Epworth men had been in prison a year through rector Rev James Gardiner, on charges connected to fines of less than four shillings, and were then committed to Fleet Prison in London. In 1673 three Epworth men and James Parnel of Haxey were all sent to prison again at the behest of James Gardiner for refusing to pay Easter offerings. Gardiner was a persistent persecutor of Quakers.

Epworth was the birthplace of the Puritan Richard Bernard (see Worksop) and the Puritan St Paul family held land here. A sign of the Baptists' strength is 'Dipping House Farm' at nearby Belton – Baptists were often called 'dippers' and this location was a popular site for immersions; it's also been said that the farm was used by candidates to prepare for dipping. In 1782 Dan Taylor baptised five and 'delivered a discourse at the water-side to a crowd of very attentive spectators'. There is also a legend – widely circulated in the 1800s – that John Smyth himself was actually first baptised by 'Elder John Morton' in the 'River Don' two miles from Epworth, to which he walked in his wet clothes – this supposedly happening in 1606. It is a lovely story, but no historian takes it seriously; it is unlikely that Smyth would have kept such a momentous decision quiet for the rest of his life. This story is explained further under Crowle.

So Samuel Wesley (1662-1735), the father of Charles and John, arrived in an unhappy town. Coming from a nonconformist background, he had veered towards the Church of England at university and by 1688 was a clergyman – the year he married Susannah Annesley, daughter of a 'silenced' clergyman who had herself turned away from nonconformity at thirteen. By 1691 he held South Ormsby in east Lincolnshire, which he felt 'a mean cot composed of reeds and clay', but resigned in 1694 after refusing to let a nobleman's mistress socialise with his wife.

Samuel Wesley's parish church at Epworth. (Author)

In 1695 his Royalist sympathies and intellectual approach were badly out of step in Epworth. A Tory, he was rector of a parish with a long hatred of the Crown due to the draining of the Carrs and a strong nonconformist tradition; he did not have the temperament for such a place, nor did he have the friends to secure him preferment elsewhere.

A lively old print of the famous rescue from the burning rectory at Epworth in 1709. (Author's collection)

His wife Susannah had a deep and reflective faith, which had an abiding influence on her children and she seemed more in step with the type of faith then common in Axholme through nonconformist influence.

Susannah Wesley has sometimes been portrayed as the paragon of Christian virtue against an irascible husband. Her husband's frequent trips away and brief visits to debtors' prison allowed her some freedom, and she is famous for kitchen prayer meetings and her guide to raising children; the first of these is clearly influential still in Christianity, the second is still popular in some parts of the world although parts are controversial.

She is often seen as the key influence, but both parents brought a fierce intellectual commitment to faith that John especially shared in.

There has been a tendency to emphasise the dramatic aspects of the Wesley parents and the faults of Samuel in particular. Yet he was able to share his spiritual thoughts with John when he was dying and the communicants at his church increased five-fold during his ministry. He was forward-looking in 1702, when he formed a religious society at Epworth divided into groups of twelve men and endeavoured to get a Christian school running.

John and Charles Wesley grew up as part of a large family in the rectory. John was born in 1703 and Charles in 1707. Famously, they nearly died (John especially was in danger) in 1709 when the rectory caught fire. Both brothers went through university and were ordained, John becoming curate at Wroot in 1728.

Back at Oxford, John began organising the 'Holy Club', which was to evolve into the Methodists. In 1735-8 he had an unsuccessful trip to America, but was impressed by the faith of the Moravians and pursued an interest in them for several years. In May 1738 he experienced a profound spiritual awakening, sometimes referred to as his 'conversion', and from 1739, under the influence of George Whitefield, he began preaching in the open air – with great success. As revival accelerated, Wesley found his position as a Church of England clergyman quite a challenge: whereas some clergy invited him to preach in their churches, others turned him away and tried to prevent his open-air preaching. Yet his success in winning souls for Christ was undeniable. At times the revival was characterised by supernatural gifts and manifestations, with some similarities to more recent patterns such as the Toronto events in the 1990s. Only after his death did Methodism separate from the Church of England.

From the 1770s, Methodism increasingly spread overseas and made significant inroads in America and into Africa. Preachers like George Shadford, of Scotter, took the message abroad. It is now perhaps more important in Nigeria, South Korea and other countries than it is in Britain – Wesley truly started a movement that has become worldwide.

Charles began with preaching to condemned prisoners and then also preaching in the open air, although he ceased to be a travelling preacher in 1756. He was really a poet who also wrote hymns, although his success as a hymn writer has perhaps overshadowed his early contributions to the success of Methodism in general.

The most famous place in Epworth is probably the tomb of Samuel Wesley in the parish graveyard. In 1742 Wesley's first visit to Epworth for many years started encouragingly, probably at the *Red Lion*:

The 'old' old Rectory at Epworth - from before it burnt down. (Author's collection)

The rebuilt Rectory at Epworth (Author's collection)

'It being many years since I had been in Epworth before, I went to an inn in the middle of the town, not knowing whether there were any left in it now who would not be ashamed of my acquaintance. But an old servant of my father's, with two or three poor women, presently found me out. I asked her, "Do you know any in Epworth who are in earnest to be saved?" She answered, "I am, by the grace of God; and I know I am saved through faith." I asked, "Have you then the peace of God? Do you know that He has forgiven your sins?" She replied, "I thank God I know it well. And many here can say the same thing"'.

Wesley attended church in the morning to hear the curate Romley preach but his tone was bitter about 'enthusiasm' and John was denied either preaching or reading prayers, so he preached from family property - his father's tomb. Romley had assisted his father and been a schoolmaster and, briefly, the hopeful admirer of one of the Wesley sisters.

'Accordingly at six I came and found such a congregation as I believe Epworth never saw before. I stood near the east end of the church, upon my father's tombstone, and cried, "The kingdom of heaven is not meat and drink; but righteousness, and peace, and joy in the Holy Ghost".'

Despite this, Wesley heard Romley preach several times, always with little joy; apparently Romley later lost his voice so few could hear him, and became a 'tippler'. He went mad in 1751 and died a few weeks later.

Wesley was on better terms with Rev John Hay, the rector, who occasionally visited during the summer. Hay shared the Lord's Supper with Wesley in

1748, whereas Romley had refused it. It seems likely that Romley's dislike of Wesley was personal and professional as much as spiritual; Romley was a local man with no hope of preferment, lacking Wesley's connections and skills, perhaps doomed to eke out his living as a schoolmaster and curate under a part-time rector who was the third son of an earl. A similar pattern was evident in later years when in 1780 the rector, Sir William Anderson, instructed the curate to allow Wesley to preach.

The most famous spot in Epworth - where John Wesley preached from a position on his father's tomb. (Boston Borough Council)

John Wesley returned to Epworth every two years or so; he preached in the town around seventy times in all. On 9 June 1755 he preached 'at the Cross' and 'great was our glorying in the Lord'. It was not always an easy place to get to: on 11 March 1758 he was coming back from Bawtry, but those sent from Epworth to meet him had already gone. In appalling conditions, he was guided through flood waters by Richard Wright, 'who knew the road over the Moor perfectly well' from 'Idlestop'. On 12 March he then preached in Epworth market place and on 13th 'in the shell of the new house' before leaving for York.

In July 1774 he had a 'numerous and quiet congregation' in the market place. In July 1776 'God struck with the hammer of his word and broke the hearts of stone', after which there was a 'love fast' at which 'the flame was soon kindled' because of one man's personal testimony. This was followed in 1779 by 'so general an outpouring of God's spirit we had seldom known'.

In 1781 efforts made through domestic prayer meetings spilled out in a spiritual revival with individuals having visionary dreams and falling to the floor. According to the account of Thomas Saxton, the revival of 1781-2 started in the factories:

'We have in Epworth three factories for spinning yarn, and weaving coarse linen cloth: the children employed here, both boys and girls, were the most profligate in the town ……Some of the girls at the largest factory sent and desired me to come to them; but I did not go. They then went to Ann Towris and Ann Field, who went to them many times, and spared no pains in talking to them. Awhile after I went to one factory myself, and saw the fruit of their labour; all the children being greatly changed, and most of them rejoicing in God. There is a great change in the other two factories also, many of the children having the saving knowledge of God'.

Alexander Kilham was one of the converts at this time (see below). In May 1782 Wesley was delighted with the progress in Epworth:

'The huge congregation was in the market place at Epworth, and the Lord in the midst of them. The love feast which followed exceeded all. I have never known such a one as here before. As soon as one had done speaking, another began. Several of them were children but they spoke with the wisdom of the aged, though with the fire of youth. So out of the mouths of babes and sucklings did God perfect praise'.

In three of the factories 'God had put a new song in their mouth' and 'religion had taken deep root in them'. However, when he returned in 1784 Wesley found that the factories had closed and some of the young people had drifted from God.

In June 1784 at a sermon at the market place 'it seemed as if very few, if any, of the sinners then present were unmoved'. In July there were more people than ever: 'great was the Holy One of Israel in the midst of them' Wesley noted. Wesley arrived in 1788 to find hardly anyone attending the church; this he felt was due to the curate Gibson's lack of piety and failure to preach the truth so that Methodists would not attend, but by then Wesley was a grand old man; when he preached at the Market Place, Wesley

John Wesley preaching in a rather formal setting - in his early days of open air preaching things were often rather less calm! (Author's collection)

seemed almost disappointed there were no longer any 'mockers'; indeed, 'all appeared as serious as death', though they cheered up at the Love Feast that followed!

However, returning in 1790 he was greatly disappointed in the Methodist Society's lack of zeal and activity. He was still able to join Mr Gibson's congregation for the afternoon service; Gibson read the prayers 'with unusual solemnity' and Wesley noted that attendance was five times greater than normal, with ten times as many taking communion. The great man preached at the Market Place again 'to such a congregation as was never seen at Epworth before'.

Epworth was not so safe for all others. One of Wesley's preachers, Mr Downes, was arrested by the constable while preaching, sent to the justices at Kirton, and from there pressed into military service via Lincoln Gaol. In Wesley's view the 'honourable men' had decided this because he was a preacher.

Methodism separated from the Church of England only after Wesley's death. By the late 1790s there was some discontent at the running of Methodism, which focused around one of its ministers, Alexander Kilham (1762-1798). He was also from Epworth, and is said to have lived at Prospect House (79 High Street). He was brought up in a Methodist family but 'the Devil often suggested to me that it was too soon to think about religion', so he became a wayward youth. When he was thirteen George Shadford visited their house and 'his conversation about the things of eternity affected me in such an extraordinary manner, that I could not refrain from weeping'. But yet again he wandered, though his father never gave up hope.

Kilham was much impressed by a neighbour's dream, in which his seven sons and daughters - 'all of whom were willing subjects of Satan's kingdom' - were cast down into the abyss; the old neighbour told them the dream and several of them turned to God. Revival was going on in Epworth, and three young ladies persuaded Kilham to join them at a meeting. Kilham spent four hours weeping before 'my heart was filled with unspeakable joy'. Amazingly, a third party account of his conversion has been discovered:

> 'Almost as soon as he came in, he was struck to the heart; and the same night he knew all his sins were forgiven. Immediately he began to go from house to house, all round the neighbourhood, speaking to everyone he met, of the things of God, and exhorting them to flee from the wrath to come. But, not content with this, he, with two or three young lads, went to several of the neighbouring towns, and were the means of kindling the same fire in almost every place where they went'.

Kilham became an active Methodist and went with Robert Carr Brackenbury to establish Methodism in Jersey. He was expelled from the Methodist Conference in 1796 and set up the New Connexion in 1798. Thereafter, Wesleyans often had a poor view of him; James Everett likened Kilham to a horsefly 'which invariably passes over the sound part of the animal and instinctively finds its way to a sore spot, upon which it feeds and which it always irritates'.

After the death of his first wife he brought his daughter Sarah to live with her grandfather at Epworth, while he travelled. This was the time of the split in the Methodists for which Kilham was blamed.

Kilham died in 1798 still very young, his last words being 'Tell all the world that Jesus is precious'. His daughter was only ten and his second wife, Hannah, was pregnant at the time of his death. The fatherless family returned to Epworth in 1800.

There was a bitter split in Epworth itself. In 1803 the 'Kilhamites' had to quit the old chapel they were using and met in a barn at the Kilham family's farm. The Kilhams also provided the land for the new Providence Chapel built in 1803-4 in Church Street. Surrounding villages such as Belton, Haxey, and Westwoodside had their MNC chapels as well as later Primitive and Wesleyan.

Kilham's second wife became a Quaker missionary in West Africa. His daughter Sarah also became a Quaker and in 1820 began running a Quaker school for poor girls in St Petersburg; she stayed there until her death in 1852, running the school, helping with a hospital and doing work for the Bible Society.

In 1861 the American Methodist evangelist Phoebe Palmer was invited to Epworth for a few days, to win souls and raise finance. She stayed at Rose Villa and toured all the scenes connected with Wesley. Although she described one female convert, Mrs Palmer seems not to have been over-impressed: '...the work has not been as general thus far as we are accustomed to witness when not blended with secular matters'.

Rev David Leese, a modern day Epworth minister, stands in Wesley's footsteps. (Author)

There was a large 'tea meeting' which she commented on as a favourite way of raising money in England, and then she departed for Crowle, which was much more to her liking.

The Methodists were re-united in 1932, largely adapting Kilham's views on governance. The Kilham chapel was closed for worship in 1944 and is currently used as a Youth Centre. It is located immediately opposite the Wesley Memorial Methodist Church.

- *Visit the tomb of Samuel Wesley, from which John famously preached.*

- *Take a walk in the churchyard as John Wesley did in July 1779. Reflect on his thoughts that day: '"One generation goeth, and another cometh." See how the earth drops its inhabitants as the tree drops its leaves.'*

- *Visit the kitchen at the Old Rectory Museum and reflect on how Susannah's 'house group' methods have influenced Christian growth worldwide.*

- *Stand at the cross in the Market Place and read from the Journals about the great things that happened there – then have lunch at the Red Lion where John often stayed.*

Epworth: Axholme (Melwood) Priory

The site of this Carthusian monastery can be found on a country road between Epworth and Owston Ferry. The Carthusian priory was founded in 1395-96 for a prior and twelve monks by Thomas Mowbray, Earl of Nottingham, at the site of a small twelfth century Premonstratensian chapel dedicated to St Mary. Augustine Webster was the prior of this monastery from 1531 and was one of a Nottinghamshire deputation who protested against the policies of Henry VIII and Thomas Cromwell, refusing to take the Oath of Supremacy, for which he was executed in 1535. Webster was canonised in 1970. The monastery was closed in June 1538.

Everton:

The church has a strange carving of horses or dragons over its doorway (a tympanum) which may be Viking in origin; it is a reminder – like the one at Austerfield – that the early Christians acted in a multi-faith culture as we do today.

This parish was home to the Drew family of Harwell, which in 1607 included three strongly Puritan brothers. John Drew was arrested for non-attendance at his parish church and by 1609 had left for the Netherlands.

Richard Clyfton's brother John was an Everton yeoman and for a time a churchwarden. By 1607 he had lost his warden's post but was in open dispute with the vicar saying he 'cared not' about being excommunicated. A new warden, Edward Rayne, also went off to join in 'secret assemblies' so that the vicar demanded action against both Clyftons.

Fillingham:

John Wycliffe held the living at Fillingham in about 1361-8, but it is not known if he ever visited it; for three of the years he was granted a licence for non-residence. Wycliffe's ideas about the Church spread through the preaching of the Lollards and into Europe. Argument has raged over his influence on the Reformation but he is, without doubt, a theologian and reformer of the first rank – whether he set foot in Fillingham or not!

Quakers here were persecuted. Thomas Bromby was a labourer who was turned out of his house in 1657 on the actions of Ralph Hollingsworth, the priest. Bromby's gaoler declared that 'all in all her years at the prison she had never known a man use more spite than the priest did to this poor man'. He died there in 1658.

John Wycliffe, 'the morning star of the Reformation'. (Author's collection)

The small church at Fillingham was the responsibility of John Wycliffe, the early reformer, but he may never have even set foot here. (Author)

Fledborough:

Rev William Sweetapple, who held Fledborough from 1712, oversaw an extraordinary increase in weddings; they increased from one every three years to twenty a year, although the village population was only sixty. It is assumed that Sweetapple was running his own version of Gretna Green in the Trent Valley.

An influential figure throughout the nineteenth century was 'Mrs Markham', author of one of the best-selling history books of the century. In fact, she was born as Elizabeth Cartwright in 1779, with a father who was a clergyman and inventor of textile machinery, and an uncle who was a famous radical politician; both of these were born nearby in Marnham.

After living in Marnham for a while, in 1814 she married a clergyman, John Penrose, who seems to have been something of a 'pluralist', holding simultaneous livings in Cornwall, at Fledborough and Thorney in Nottinghamshire (both near Marnham), and Bracebridge and Langton-by-Wragby in Lincolnshire. He had more or less inherited Fledborough from his father, who had been presented to it by the Duchess of Kingston upon Hull, a distant relative.

Elizabeth, dissatisfied with available history books to read to her children, published 'A History of England from the First Invasion by the Romans to the End of the Reign of George III' in 1823. The book was hugely successful – it was possibly the best-selling history book of the century – but was later much lampooned for its view of 'good' and 'bad' people and for a rather Anglican view of history – '1066 and all that' being the classic 'spoof.'

John Penrose senior's sister Mary (1791-1873) married the famous Dr Thomas Arnold, headmaster of Rugby School and pioneer of 'muscular Christianity'. One of their sons was Matthew Arnold, the famous poet, whose poem *Dover Beach* portrays the withdrawal of Christian faith. This must make Mrs Markham the best connected vicar's wife in our book.

Elizabeth Penrose of Fledborough became a famous 'historical' author. (Author)

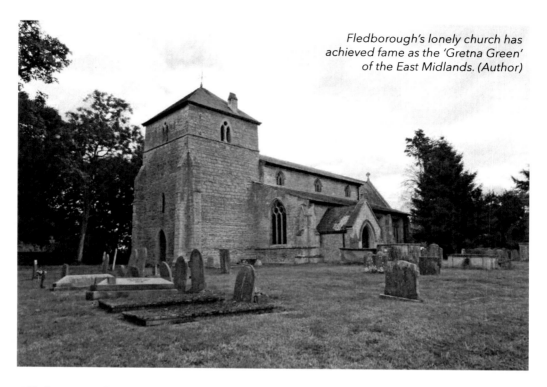

Fledborough's lonely church has achieved fame as the 'Gretna Green' of the East Midlands. (Author)

Flixborough:

One of the rectors, Jonathan Grant, was held prisoner in four different castles during the Civil War and his wife became a Baptist. In 1662 he was one of the clergy who was silenced and he moved away.

Henry Waterland, the rector here and also in Walesby (far enough away to be inconvenient!) was the father of Daniel Waterland (1683-1740), who became Master of Magdalene College and also an influential theologian.

Frodingham:

John Ryther was a Yorkshireman with Quaker parents who during the Civil War period managed to become vicar of Frodingham. He was ejected from here in 1660, then 'silenced' in 1662 while at North Ferriby, and – after a brief visit to York Gaol – began a church there. In 1668 he started one in Bradford and later another Congregational one in Wapping; nowadays we might say he was a 'church planter'. In Wapping he had a place at the centre of British merchant shipping and he adapted his preaching for this audience, becoming known as the 'Seaman's Preacher', using a style 'adapted to their situation and taste'. The seamen repaid his help by sheltering him when he was at risk of arrest. Arguably this was the first-ever seamen's mission.

Gainsborough:

In 873 the Viking army wintered at nearby Torksey and from 1003 Gainsborough was Sweyn Forkbeard's 'capital' in England. Sweyn died here in 1014, and an oft-told legend is that he was struck down by the spirit of Saint Edmund on account of his plundering of English churches. Apparently in 1013 Ailwin, custodian of Edmund's shrine, had a vision in which Edmund warned Sweyn to leave the English people alone. Edmund clearly intended Ailwin to deliver the message in person to Sweyn. Ailwin hesitated, until as 1014 dawned Sweyn increased the pressure by demanding extra 'taxes' from the monks.

Florence of Worcester says Sweyn was struck down by Edmund just after planning a raid on his shrine, whilst John of Tinmouth said that Edmund's ghost stabbed him as he sat in a chair. William of Malmesbury related that Sweyn was struck down in his sleep for 'answering rudely' back to Edmund! The most likely explanation is that Sweyn was poisoned, but however he died it was certainly a great day in Gainsborough's history!

His successor Cnut was a Christian, albeit one whose 'piety was of a very ostentatious type.' So the famous story of him turning back the waves may have been about 'proving' his humility – for of course it was his courtiers who believed he could turn back the waves, not Cnut. Some claims have even been made that this happened at Gainsborough, with Cnut attempting to stop the passage of the 'Aegir', the Trent tidal bore.

Katherine Parr is most famous for being Henry VIII's last wife, but long before that in May 1529 she married Edward Borough (or Burgh), son of Thomas, the 3rd baron Burgh of Gainsborough.

The Trent was an important routeway for the Vikings and Gainsborough their capital, but within two generations they were Christians. (Author's collection)

Her first father-in-law was 'an overbearing bully whose children lived in fear of his temper' and in 1530 Katherine and her husband escaped to the manor at Kirton in Lindsey. When she married her second husband she became trapped at Snape by rebels against Henry.

After her second husband's death Katherine lived at the royal court, where she hoped to marry Thomas Seymour but, through family politics, instead received the offer she could not refuse – marriage to Henry VIII. Her 'zealous evangelical' faith won her enemies, including Stephen Gardiner, the powerful Bishop of Winchester, who tried to force evidence against her from Anne Askew, the Lincolnshire martyr. Katherine was the first queen of England to produce a book herself: *The Lamentation of a Sinner* in 1547. She survived the death of Henry.

Robert Browne, a Stamford man, was one of the first 'Separatists.' A 'Brownist' group seems to have formed at Gainsborough and perhaps influenced John Smyth when he arrived here. It is possible that Smyth preached in the town in 1604. A Brownist was also said to have influenced Hanserd Knollys, who became a famous Baptist preacher, when he was living in Gainsborough.

Sir William Hickman bought the manor and the Old Hall in 1596; the Hickmans were Protestants of the finest vintage. Hickman's grandfather was said to have smuggled Gospels into England during Henry VIII's time and his parents, Anthony and Rose, had sheltered Bishop John Hooper, John Knox and John Foxe at the time of Queen Mary. Anthony was imprisoned in 1554; then they had lived in exile in Antwerp.

William was not always on good terms with all the local Puritans and had a legal dispute with Sir William Wray and his friend St Paul after the death of a Hickman servant in 1598.

John Smyth, who had attended school in Gainsborough, was here in 1604 and in March 1606 he 'prophesyed' at the parish church in the absence of the vicar (but at the invitation of the congregation) and got into legal trouble; Gervase Helwys and William Hickman signed letters of support showing that both were still of puritan leanings. Smyth became 'pastor' of a congregation at Gainsborough at least by autumn 1607, formally breaking from the Church of England. He was criticised for being 'made minister by tradesmen' but it was a momentous step by a strong-minded individual. William Bradford later referred to 'two distinct bodies': Gainsborough and Scrooby were individual churches.

In 1608 some Separatist 'Pilgrims' left Gainsborough. Thomas Helwys hired the *Francis* to collect the women and children at Gainsborough while most of the men walked to Stallingborough Creek. Stallingborough was home of the Askews who were a well-connected family. However, the plan was discovered

Thomas Cooper: preacher, politician, atheist, convert, poet - how many have led such a full and varied life? (Author's collection)

by the authorities, so most of the women and children were left behind. In one account, the women and children asked to stay overnight and sheltered in Immingham church. This allowed the authorities time to capture them. Those on the Dutch vessel endured a stormy fourteen-day passage. Robinson, Clyfton and Brewster seem to have arrived in Amsterdam after this, in August 1608.

In Holland, Smyth and then Helwys were baptised, splitting them permanently from the Clyfton-Robinson-Brewster congregation.

John Murton, from Gainsborough, sided with Helwys when he split with Smyth in 1610 before both returned to England around 1611, which Helwys saw as their Christian duty.

This earned Murton the enmity of Robinson, who later condemned him as 'better suited for wielding a shovel and a pick than for discussing theology'. Yet modern critics see him as 'quite able to hold more than shovel and pick'.

Helwys and Murton were soon in Newgate; Helwys died by early 1616 and Murton spent most of the time until 1626 there. He wrote at least two works there, with *A Most Humble Supplication* (1620) apparently written in milk as there was no ink, then smuggled out to friends who read it by firelight. Murton argued that a true church consisted only of baptised believers who had repented and 'publicly confessed their faith in Christ' – so babies, who had neither sinned nor repented, did not need baptism.

Murton also developed Helwys's thinking on religious freedom and the separation of spiritual from more political authority. Addressing the king he wrote, 'It is not in your power to compel the heart; you may compel men to be hypocrites, as a great many are, who are false-hearted towards God and the state, which is sin both in you and them'. In his 1615 work, *Objections answered by way of dialogue*, Murton said that it was 'heinous…to force men and women by cruel persecutions, to bring their bodies to a worship whereunto they cannot bring their spirits'. Murton said history would judge on the issue of compulsion in religion:

'Will not succeeding ages cry out against the cruelty of the learned Protestants herein, as well as they cry out against the cruelty of the learned Jews and papists? Yes, we are assured they will, as many millions do in other nations this day'.

Murton also separated spiritual and earthly wisdom: 'The Spirit bloweth where it listeth and is not tied to learning'. He disagreed with the view that the Holy Spirit only spoke to educated clerics; in Murton's view, the key 'offices' were of preaching, then 'reading and interpreting'. He was explicitly spiritual in advocating a freedom in worship: 'Worship Him with our souls and our spirits, and…according to the truth of his Word.' In *A description of what God hath predestinated* in 1620, he roundly criticised the Calvinist views on predestination. He could not imagine anything 'more repugnant to the nature of God' than that men were sent to hell for doing the things God might have compelled them to do.

Murton died in about 1625 or 1626, but within a few years the Baptist Church was firmly rooted in England. The ideas of Helwys and Murton were later found in Roger Williams, a Puritan who married the daughter of Richard Bernard (see Worksop) and migrated to New England.

The true effigies of the late Reverend Divi Mr HANSERD KNOLLIS. Ætatis suæ 93.

Hanserd Knollys was set on his way by an 'old Brownist' of Gainsborough.

He knew Hanserd Knollys, another influential early Baptist, who at Cambridge had come under Puritan influence, before returning to his home county to teach at Gainsborough. There he attended 'Brownist' meetings where the believer used to 'pray and expand scriptures in his family'. In America, Knollys was embroiled in controversy, before returning to have some success in England. Meanwhile, there was a Baptist group in the town by about 1640.

George Fox the Quaker arrived in 1651 and his preaching 'caused an uproar'. In 1652 one of the 'Friends' preached in the market place and again there was 'uproar'; Fox went into a friend's house but a crowd chased him, accusing him of preaching that he was the Messiah.

Fox accused the accuser of being a Judas, and won over the hearts of the crowd; his accuser went away cowed and later hung himself and a stake was apparently driven through his grave.

Under Charles II, William Hickman was an active persecutor of Quakers and informers were rewarded with a third of any fines levied. Quakers here established their own burial ground in 1668 at Kexby; in the 1700s, a third of Lincolnshire Quakers belonged to the Gainsborough congregation.

Presbyterian or Congregationalist ideas were strong in the town through the years of persecution. Matthew Coates was in trouble for his dissenting views in 1663-4, but he was eventually able to have his house licensed for meetings and it was still in use in 1690; by 1701 he had given land for a meeting house built in Ratton Row. More recently, the John Robinson Memorial Church was opened in 1897 as a Congregational Church, with significant funding from America as part of the Pilgrims' Tercentenary celebrations.

John Wesley preached here regularly, including in Sir Neville Hickman's Old Hall. In August 1759 he preached to 'a rude, wild multitude (a few of a better spirit excepted)' but largely won them over; afterwards the crowd was astonished when Sir Neville congratulated Wesley on his sermon. In August 1761 he was in the Old Hall again with 'a mixed multitude, part civil, part rude as bears'.

George Shadford wrote that he attended regular Methodist services at 1.30pm in the Old Hall, in 1761. In 1766 Wesley noted Hickman's help in protecting the Methodists at Scotter.

Wesley preached in several places in Gainsborough - here are two of the early ones. (Author's collection)

Photo: Mr. F. T. Shipham.]
MR. DEAN'S CHAPEL.

Photo: Mr. F. T. Shipham.]
THE HIRED ROOM IN THE WHITE HORSE YARD, GAINSBOROUGH.

In 1788 Wesley preached at
Gainsborough in 'our new house.'
(Author's collection)

Photo : Mr. F. T. Shipham.]   [By favour of Mr. J. Barlow

"OUR NEW HOUSE AT GAINSBOROUGH."

He preached in 1779 and in June 1780 he preached twice and enjoyed a 'love feast'; 'many spoke, and with great fervour, as well as simplicity'. In 1781 and in 1784 he was allowed to use 'Mr Dean's Chapel' to good effect; 'possibly some good may be done even at Gainsborough!' he concluded. In 1786 he preached in 'Sir Neville Hickman's Yard' and lamented Sir Neville's death and the decay of the buildings, but in 1788 was able to preach in 'our new House'; he was in the town again in 1790, where he hoped the Society was recovering from being 'miserably depressed'. It was not always the crowd that was the problem:

> 'Friday, 6 April [1764] – I preached at Ferry at nine in the morning, and in the evening; and, about noon, in Sir N. H.'s hall at Gainsborough. Almost as soon as I began to speak, a cock began to crow over my head; but he was quickly dislodged, and the whole congregation, rich and poor, were quiet and attentive'.

In the late 1700s the Church of England clergy reported 250 Methodists in the town – much the largest return in Lincolnshire. We rarely get insights into how difficult the work of the travelling preachers was, but the Journal of Thomas

Edman (of Horncastle) tells us a little of preaching in 1794; having been to Burton Stather, where the 'lady of the house' did not like his preaching, he then preached at Gainsborough:

> 'What poor work did I make in the pulpit last night, how was I dissatisfied therewith. I cannot tell how the people would like (it). And what I am to do I cannot tell for I seem as tho' I cannot get nothing fresh! Oh, Lord if thou hast called me to the work of the ministry qualify me for the same'.

Emily Wesley, John's sister, ran a school in Gainsborough around 1735 and her mother Susannah may have stayed with her for a while after Samuel Wesley's death. John Simpson (1709-1766) was born in Gainsborough and was a close associate of the Wesleys in the Oxford 'Holy Club'; however, he left Methodism and joined the Moravian Ockbrook group; then he descended into alcohol problems – a sad story of wasted potential.

Thomas Middleton (1769-1822) became curate of Gainsborough in 1792, a role he combined with editing the weekly *Country Spectator*. In 1814 he became Bishop of Calcutta, a role which attracted the princely salary of £5000. Once there, Middleton took the view that Indians were 'not ready for the Bible', but in 1820 he started work on a mission college. In the view of his biographer, he 'laid the foundations on which others could build'.

The Primitive Methodists brought revival times back to Gainsborough in 1818 starting, according to Thomas Cooper's account, with two men (William Braithwaite and Thomas Saxton) singing aloud in the streets. Soon they were able to take over the old Wesleyan chapel in Little Church Lane. Cooper recalled fervent prayer meetings lasting until midnight and 'many up-grown sinners professed to find the pardon of their sins'. He recalled a notorious gambler, 'an inveterate cock-fighting man, who converted and remained true to his faith for the rest of his life', but there were also 'some fearful backslidings'. A convert of 1820, W G Bellham, gives a personal account of responding to a preacher: 'I never saw so much of God in a man before; he was all love; and every word he uttered was to my soul like honey dropping from the honeycomb. I felt so happy in my own soul, that I thought I could live and die with these people'.

George Rex was the leading light, holding meetings at his house, 'Joppa', and was the first to sign 'the pledge'. In 1835-6 some travelling preachers staying there experienced a malign supernatural weight upon them. Later he led the church in Retford.

One of the most famous Baptists of the era was Thomas Cooper. He was a shoemaker in Gainsborough, where he joined the Methodists and became a lay preacher. He taught himself to read widely – he could recite thousands of lines of poetry, knew seven Shakespeare plays by heart, and learnt Greek and Latin. However, he most loved *The Pilgrim's Progress* and called it his 'book of books'. With a friend, he set up a Sunday school, which soon attracted five hundred children and adults. Then Cooper, still only twenty-two, opened a day school.

He met his wife, Susanna, in Lincoln in 1829. However, his school ran into problems. Some of Cooper's energy went into night-time prayer meetings of over five hours or itinerant preaching, but he fell out with the local Methodist Superintendent, Jonathan Williams, who he accused of feasting whilst pretending to be too ill to preach. Williams engineered Cooper's suspension. Cooper was, nonetheless, an effective preacher and his sermons 'often reduced his audience to tears'.

Cooper became a journalist in Lincoln, criticising the cathedral staff, then became a Chartist agitator. In Leicester he was leader of the Adult School, a preacher and political agitator, and in and out of prison in the 1840s including for a speech that sparked a miners' riot in Staffs. He then fell out with other Chartist leaders – a common pattern.

He made a living lecturing to radical and 'free-thought' audiences upon educational subjects. While addressing one of these audiences in 1856, he suddenly broke off and announced that he had been reconverted to the truths of Christianity. Former supporters were outraged, and Cooper wrote to his

The centre of Gainsborough in 1830 where Primitive Methodists were adept at attracting attention.

friend Charles Kingsley that 'God has been so good to me that I must confess Christ, and we shall have greater rage now that I have come to Christianity'.

In 1858 he experienced a miraculous escape from a train disaster and decided to devote his life to God. He became a Baptist after discussion at Barnsley, and was baptised in Leicester in 1859. He gave 3300 lectures and sermons, living nowhere – eventually his wife gave up and went to live with relatives after six years of travelling.

Thomas Cooper died on 15 July 1892 in Lincoln. His grave was restored in 1993 and a church in Lincoln named in his honour.

- *Gainsborough Old Hall – a fantastic building in its own right, it may have links to the Pilgrims but we can be certain that Wesley preached here several times.*
- *The John Robinson Memorial Church.*
- *The Quaker Meeting House at 22 Market Street.*

Gamston:

This Baptist church was founded probably in 1690 by Aaron Jeffery. Jeffery worked on the domestic staff of the Earl of Clare who was impressed by his 'General Baptist' character. Before there was a church at Gamston, Jeffery would walk twelve miles to Collingham on a Sunday where he sometimes

An artist's impression of what the original Gamston Baptist chapel might have looked like.

preached whilst wearing his gold 'livery'. Famously, his employer lent him a horse to help ease his journeys.

After he left service, Jeffery rented a farm at Gamston and began to hold meetings there – thus the Baptist church evolved. Jeffery and his wife died within hours of each other in 1729.

Dan Taylor (1738-1816) was a Yorkshireman whose conversion to the Baptists led to a significant revival in this denomination; he created the Baptist 'New Connection' in 1770. Taylor was a miner who was briefly a Methodist but had doubts about Wesley's leadership and left in 1762. He founded his own small group at Wadsworth and came to accept believers' baptism. However, when he sought out Baptist ministers who would baptise him he found they refused because of his belief that 'Jesus tasted death for every man, and made a propitiation for the sins of the world'. Taylor was an Arminian, surrounded by Calvinists.

Taylor and his friend Slater set out for the church in Boston, passing through Gamston to Tuxford along the Great North Road. They stopped where there was a 'decent inn' and discovered there was a Baptist deacon in the village, but they got a cool reception from him. The next day they retraced their steps to Gamston, having met Mr Dossey, a deacon, conducting a service. They were welcomed in by Mr Jeffery, the pastor, in whose house they stayed for three days. There they learnt about the 'Old Connexion' church at Gamston, the General Baptists and the Lincolnshire Association.

Taylor was baptised in the River Idle at Gamston in February 1763 by Jeffery. Slater opted to delay his own baptism so that Taylor could do it later. This made Gamston 'a place of some celebrity in General Baptist history'. Taylor then went back to Wadsworth and baptised others before, in May 1763, formalising his links with other Baptists. With support from Boston, Taylor formed the first General Baptist church in Yorkshire and Dossey was one of the first preachers. However, some doctrinal differences emerged and in 1765 Taylor met with others at Gamston to debate issues such as the laying-on of hands.

In 1770 Taylor was instrumental in forming the New Connexion of General Baptists. This had a significant impact in reviving the General Baptist strand, which became strong in Nottinghamshire.

It is possible that the last Nottinghamshire outdoor baptisms to be conducted in 'old' times were held in the River Idle, most likely at Gamston. The last reported was 1881. Outdoor baptism seems to have declined after a Mormon minister was prosecuted following a drowning in Cheshire.

- *Taylor was baptised near the current bridge over the Idle - an historic place for Baptists.*

Gateford:

John Lassells (Lascelles) of Gateford and Sturton was employed by Chancellor Thomas Cromwell in 1538, having lost his previous post because of his evangelical views; in a classic example of evangelical connections, this was arranged by his guardian, Sir John Hercy of Grove. His brother George worked for Cromwell in the dissolution of Lenton. In 1539 John secured a post in the King's household where he found others with similar religious views. In 1540 Lassells cautioned his friends as, after Cromwell's fall, the Howards and Bishop Gardiner were in the ascendancy. Then Lassells' sister, Mary Hall, told him about the sexual antics of Queen Catherine Howard in her youth, and Lassells passed this to Cranmer - leading to the downfall of the Howards.

George acquired the manor of Sturton where the family already held land in 1540 after its previous lord, Thomas Darcy, was executed following the Lincolnshire Rising; Sturton was to be central to the story of the Pilgrims.

Gradually Lassells grew less cautious about his faith, becoming involved with the radical Anne Askew. One historian of the reformation, Dickens, considers Lassells to have been a key figure amongst the court evangelicals - which included Katherine Parr. He was arrested in the middle of 1546 and professed his willingness to die for his beliefs. He was a firm opponent of the Mass and wrote a defence on his position from his cell: 'The Masse is the vnquietnes of all Christendome, a blasphemy vnto Christes bloud, and a shame to all Christen Princes'. Lassells took the view that the words of Jesus, 'this is my body,' were misunderstood - it having been falsely assumed that he meant the bread in his hand rather than the body itself in which he dwelt.

Askew and Lassells were burnt along with two others at Smithfield. (Author's collection)

In the Tower Lassells feared that Anne Askew had repudiated her beliefs, having been tortured. He wrote to her, and she replied: 'O friend, most dearly beloved in God, I marvel not a little what should move you to judge in me so slender a faith as to fear death, which is the end of all misery. In the Lord, I desire you not to believe in me such wickedness'. When they went to the stake at Smithfield, friends attached gunpowder so they would die quickly.

- *There is a small family memorial in Worksop Priory, but nothing directly connected to John. This is a major gap in our local heritage.*

Glentworth:

In 1566 this church had some active churchwardens who gleefully reported that they had burned the rood screen with its images of Mary and John, and defaced the vestments which Mr Wray had bought. The alb had been made into a surplice and the holy water stoop defaced. The altar cloth had been made into tablecloths.

Until 1557 Glentworth was held by the Brocklesby family. Its head, Robert (d.1553) and his son Robert also died, and the lands were bequeathed in part to the latter's widow Anne, whose second husband, Sir Christopher Wray, bought the title to the rest soon after.

The Brocklesbys were prominent Puritans: Robert's brother Edward (born here) fled to Emden during the time of Mary I and they were associates of Archdeacon Bullingham, supporting him in becoming Bishop of Lincoln. By 1565 Edward was vicar of Hemel Hempstead but was the first man to be removed as part of Archbishop Parker's crackdown on nonconformity; his offences included calling the Virgin Mary 'a lump of sinne as other women are' and refusal to wear the surplice.

Isabel and Frances head the row of four sisters at the Wray memorial in Glentworth. (Janie Berry)

Edward was presented to a new living at Branston, near Lincoln, by Sir Christopher Wray – a rising lawyer – in 1568, presumably with Bullingham's support and as he held land there.

Wray embarked on a spectacular legal and political career. He was heavy-handed against Puritans and Catholics alike. He was Speaker of the Commons and Lord Chief Justice. His reputation was of a cautious, conservative man yet he produced three children who were stars of the Puritan movement. He also heavily endowed the Puritan-leaning college of Magdalene (with revenues from the parsonage at Gainsthorpe) and many Puritan ministers were trained with his money. Anne was involved in founding Kirton School in 1577 and more scholarships to Magdalene after Wray died.

The Wrays' influential Puritan children were Sir William (1560-1617), Isabel (?-1622) and Frances (?-1634). Frances is covered under Snarford, and other family members under Blyton.

By 1586 Isabel was married to her first husband, Foljambe, and was active in radical Christianity; she brought a woman said to be possessed, Katherine Wright, to her house near Chesterfield. After various ministers failed to cast out the demon, John Darrell was said to have accomplished the act. Isabel linked him with another group of Puritans under Arthur Hildersham at Ashby de la Zouch. They in turn had a network with like-minded men such as John Ireton, the rector of Kegworth 1581-1606, Thomas Helwys and Richard Bernard – whose education she had supported. In 1599 Isabel remarried, becoming Lady Bowes, expanding her interests into Durham. She continued to use the money from her family and husbands to further Puritanism and had connections to many significant Puritans in the Midlands.

Sir William and Lady Bowes supported the Millenary Petition for church reform and they expressed their views to the Earl of Shrewsbury, in 1603. Paying an unusual tribute to female spiritual insight, Sir William wrote he had consulted his wife because 'she is verie wise, especiallie in thinges of this kind'.

Sir William Wray prays at the top of his father's tomb, but he was in his own right a patron of the leading puritans including John Smyth. (Janie Berry)

Isabel heads the row of four Wray sisters, and then became a leading figure in the puritan movement for two decades or more. (Janie Berry)

Sir William then transmitted Lady Bowes's detailed criticisms of the University of Oxford's disparaging *Answer to the Millenary Petition*.

Lady Bowes added her personal postscript to the letter, comparing the *Answer* to Rabshakeh's ultimatum to Hezekiah (see 2 Kings 18: 19-36) – a comparison all the more barbed because 'railing Rabshakeh' was a stock figure of a blasphemer in religious literature. She also prayed that God would turn the King's heart and lead him to favour the Petition. Shrewsbury replied to Lady Bowes that 'your indiscrete comparison bewrayes the weaknes of your womanhode, thoughe much disagreeing from the modestie of your sex'.

Using the example of Eve, he warned Sir William against following his wife's guidance and bemoaned the influence Puritan ministers had on 'simple women'.

Isabel and her family used the Wray funds to send men like Richard Bernard to university: the Puritans wanted well-educated men in the pulpit. He preached widely in West Lindsey. Their own churches had Puritan ministers: Robert Atkinson at Glentworth in 1604 was in trouble for ignoring demands to use Prayer Book and surplice.

In 1606 Isabel and Bowes hosted the famous Puritan 'summit' at Coventry, at which the movement split into Separatists and others, the latter including all the Wrays; yet Smyth still respected her, and Helwys dedicated a book to her in 1611 (hoping to convert her to free will beliefs). It is possible she continued to meet with them at Walton, near Chesterfield, for some time after 1606. Isabel also paid for the evangelism of County Durham by Richard Rothwell. When she expressed concern as to the reception he would get, he told her, 'Madam, if I thought I should not meet the devil, I would not go: he and I have been at odds in other places, and I hope we shall not agree there'. After that, she brought him to tackle Mansfield.

Bowes died 1611 and in 1617 Isabel married Lord Darcy of Chesterfield. She died in 1622 and was buried at Rawmarsh. The text preached at her funeral

The four sisters - including two who died young - piously pray at the side of their father Sir Christopher, but it was perhaps their mother who they followed in life. (Janie Berry)

was Matthew 26.13: 'Wheresoever this Gospel shall be preached in the whole world, there shall also this, that this woman hath done be told for a memorial of her'. Rothwell's biographer wrote, 'Oh that God would raise out of the ashes of this Phoenix some more such mothers in Israel'.

Isabel's brother Sir William was an MP but he was rather denigrated in the family history as 'he does not seem to have made any figure in the world, though he brought honour to his name by two good marriages he made'. Gervase Holles described him as 'a simple honest man' and a strong Puritan. He had some direct control over eight parishes.

In politics he had limited success; when elected as MP for Grimsby in 1604 he formed an alliance with his brother in law, Sir George St Paul (or St Poll) to promote many Puritan causes - mostly with little impact. They promoted a Bill against 'scandalous and unworthy ministers' and for reform of the ecclesiastical courts.

In 1606 he was trying to win legislation on Sabbath observance and to control 'pluralities' and ministers who did not live in their parishes; he wanted legal action to ensure better educated clergy. He died in 1617. John Smyth, an 'expert witness', believed him to be the 'principal patron of godly religion in Lincolnshire' and dedicated his first book to him: 'my approved friend and benefactor'.

Glentworth was also a centre of Quakerism in the 1650s. In 1655 Richard Farnworth and Nayler met Thomas Moore and the 'Manifestarians'

Another view of the Wray sisters planning the future of Christian England...... (Janie Berry)

at Glenworth for a debate. He challenged them to fast for a fortnight on water alone and to preach without use of books! Sir Richard and probably Sir John Wray became Quakers later in the 1650s.

- *Glentworth is an essential place because the Wrays were crucial in Puritan developments; all three siblings appear on the remarkable monument to Sir Christopher in the church.*

Greasley:

The significance of Greasley, which included Beauvale in its parish, was its importance as an enclave of the north Nottinghamshire Puritan group. Not only was Beauvale held by the Disneys, and then used by the Whites of Sturton, but Thomas Helwys lived not far away in Broxtowe, and earlier the Askew family, whose daughter was martyred in 1546, held lands nearby at Nuthall.

When in 1604 John Robinson, the future leader of the Pilgrims in the Netherlands, married Bridget White at Greasley church, it was because the White family had moved to Beauvale from Sturton-le-Steeple.

In 1607 there were complaints that churchwardens had allowed the Puritan exorcist John Darrell to preach here and John Smyth also preached. In 1628 Samuel Tuke, from a significant family of Puritan clergymen, became the vicar, and during the Protectorate years Robert Smalley. Although Smalley was 'a winning preacher', he was removed in 1662 but continued to preach in the area; in 1669 meetings of around a hundred Presbyterians were taking place at a tanner's house, addressed by Smalley. He also held meetings in his own house in Mansfield. Smalley had a 'presage' of his own imminent death and so met other godly men in Mansfield to pray, apparently dying later the same day.

Gringley on the Hill

It is commonly claimed that James Brewster, brother of the pilgrim William, was 'perpetual vicar' at Gringley from 1604 until 1617, whilst also being vicar of Sutton cum Lound for much of the same period. There is some debate as to whether the two incumbents were in fact the same man or not but the fact that this James was involved in prosecuting several cases of 'abuse of clergy' against parishioners in 1611-2 might point to him being a typical puritan!

What we do know is that two significant Victorian missionaries were born in Gringley. Joseph Tindall's life is noted under Misterton, where he mainly grew up. It is a curious coincidence that the second missionary's life followed a similar pattern: born in Gringley, soon moved to Misterton, then mission in southern

Africa. Henrietta Stockdale was born here in 1847 although her father was vicar of Misterton and West Stockwith; there was no suitable house within his parish so he rented a home at Gringley, moving to Misterton only in 1850. In 1858 Mr Stockdale was presented to the living of Bole which apparently had had no vicar appointed since 1731 – being served by an occasional curate from the 1820s. This caused further housing problems: 'There was a dilapidated church, only a little dame's school, and no vicarage, so the family again took refuge in a neighbouring village, and lived in a farmhouse at Beckingham. This was a splendid place for the children; there were a lot of farm buildings where they kept rabbits and fowls, and on wet days they could play in the hay-lofts; there was also a large garden and orchard, so that when lessons were over, they found endless amusement on the premises without being any trouble or anxiety to their parents.' They only moved to Bole in 1864.

In 1863 Henrietta was inspired by stories of the Orange River Mission but it was not until her father moved to Clayworth in 1873 that she decided what to do. Soon after she moved to Bloemfontein where Henrietta became a type of Anglican nun, with a strong mission amongst women. In 1877 she moved to Kimberley – the diamond mining centre - and opened a hospital which became famous. In 1891 her work to improve nursing standards led to the first state registration of nurses anywhere in the world. There she laboured hard with only brief respites, including during the famous siege of Kimberley in the Boer War. She died in 1911.

Grove:

Grove was one of the country estates that surrounded Retford. Sir John Hercy (c1499-1570) was involved with George Lassells (see Gateford) in dissolving local priories and was the guardian of the martyr, John Lassells; he clearly knew Thomas Cromwell well and, when Mary came to the throne, his avowed Protestantism saw him lose favour. Hercy undoubtedly helped to make the Retford area a 'godly' enclave and was related through marriage to the Denmans. When Hercy died, he left the manor of West Retford to William Denman, his nephew. Grove became one of the Puritan 'livings': Francis Denman held it from 1560 to 1579, then Francis Nevill as rector until 1611 – with various Puritan curates! Hercy died without a son, so his other lands passed to the Nevilles of Ragnall.

Gervase Nevyle (Nevill) came from the Ragnall branch of this extended family and was a Separatist; he was arrested in 1607 and imprisoned in York for attending conventicles. He was 'a very dangerous schismatical separatist Brownist and irreligious subject.' He went to Holland by 1609. Nevill was probably the 'Jervis Zetwell' recorded as in the Amsterdam congregation as a box-maker. He was one of those who signed the declaration in 1609/10 as one of the remaining members of Smyth's Amsterdam congregation. Gentry families had several properties and there is confusion over where he lived: when arrested he was 'said to be of Scrooby' but with a family from Ragnall. If he was at Scrooby in 1607, this would suggest he switched to Smyth's congregation in the Netherlands. He was clearly a man on a journey, as historian M R Watts notes that by 1611 he had returned to the Church of England – perhaps even the Church of Rome.

Halton, West:

This is a very early Christian site. Æthelthryth (also 'Etheldreda') was an East Anglian princess who first married in 652 despite having taken a vow of perpetual virginity. Her husband agreed to respect this vow, but died in 655. She retired to live as a nun on the Isle of Ely but in 660, for political reasons, was married off to Ecgfrith, King of Northumbria. At first Ecgfrith also respected her vow and she was encouraged by Wilfrid, but in 672 he changed his mind and attempted to take her from her nunnery by force. She escaped and made the long journey from Northumbria to Ely, crossing the Humber to Wintringham with her maids Sewenna and Sewara. She then stayed for several days at a village called 'Alftham' (identified as here), surrounded by marshes, and constructed a church here. The 'stately, magnificent' church here was heavily damaged in a 'tempest' and was in ruins in 1696. Some claims have been made for nearby Whitton as the monastic site.

Haxey:

The church was damaged in 1626 during riots against the drainage – ironically destroying a window marking the grant of use of this land from the fourteenth century. The village was an important early centre for the Quakers. When Richard Farnworth preached here in about 1652 he reported events that 'shaketh kingdoms and turns the world upside down'.

Rev Joseph Hoole of Haxey was one of those consulted during the haunting of Epworth rectory by 'Old Jeffrey.' Later the curate here preached against John Wesley. In 1725 Hetty Wesley made her unhappy marriage to a plumber, William Wright, in this church. In 1770 John Wesley was not welcome in the church, so preached nearby. In 1774 Wesley 'had a useful sermon at Haxey church'.

The adjacent settlements of Overthorp, Newby and Westwoodside were also calling points for Wesley. When he preached in 1757 he was much encouraged that 'all the wanderers' who had been led astray fifteen years earlier had returned to the fold, including the one who misled them! In 1786 Wesley lamented how small the parish church congregation at Haxey had become and cursed the impact of plural livings on parish life since Mr 'Harle' had lived there; then he preached beneath a tree at Overthorpe. The absentee rector must have been Spencer Madan, who became Bishop of Bristol in 1792 and then Peterborough in 1794; in 1786 he held at least three benefices, one of which was near Salisbury, and was also a chaplain to the King, and a Peterborough canon – but the clue is perhaps in his first appointment, as domestic chaplain to the Duke of Chandos. Madan was a cousin of the famous poet and hymn writer William Cowper. His first wife was the daughter of an earl. He must have accumulated a considerable income, yet was said to be austere in his habits. On his tomb at Peterborough was written:

In sacred sleep the pious Bishop lies:

Say not, in death – a good man never dies.

Perhaps John Wesley might not have agreed, having seen his own father's career founder for lack of the sort of connections that Madan enjoyed.

Madan's brother Martin was actually converted under the influence of John Wesley at Oxford, abandoning a successful legal career. However, in 1780 he wrote a book advocating polygamy and a successful career as an evangelical was ruined in a moment. Theologian Matthew Horbery (1706-73) was also born here.

- *Haxey is a good place to reflect on the anger John Wesley felt about clergymen who collected the money but neglected their duties – as they lived elsewhere. The history of the Church has not always been glorious, and it needs to embrace those who are prepared to speak up when they see wrong being done.*

Hayton

The Jessops were a leading Puritan family. The first 'pastor' of the 'Pilgrims', Richard Clyfton, seems to have known them, and in 1593 was nominated as a supervisor of Richard Jessop's will; it has been suggested that Richard's brother was Francis Jessop, later to be found in a leading role with the Pilgrims at Amsterdam. One of the White sisters from Sturton, Frances, married Francis Jessop at Worksop in 1605 and went to Leiden, although he returned in the 1630s. William Jessop presented Hayton's 'very zealous' Puritan vicar Thomas Toller (who also supervised the will) to the living of Sheffield St Peter & St Paul in 1598.

Headon:

Now a tiny hamlet but from the 1590s Headon was a centre for religious radicalism held by the Wastneys family and also influenced by the Nevills at Grove, whilst land also belonged to relatives of John Robinson's wife. Religious life appears to have been chaotic: in 1589 a presentment bill concerning Headon complained that:

> Our service is not done according to the Book of Common Prayer; our church and chancel are out of repair; Edward Formary committed fornication with Frances Mynnett; Mr Hunt does not wear the surplice; Wm Harper is a usurer; Mr F. Nevyll does not bestow the 50th part of our parsonage amongst the poor.

Robert Southworth was the curate there in 1590 when he was in trouble for not wearing a surplice, and then its radical vicar from 1596, being 'deprived' in 1605 after being remarkably persistent in his nonconformity; only to be followed by another Puritan in Thomas Hancock, formerly curate of Scrooby and vicar of Elkesley. Southworth also acted as curate at Grove and apparently at Scrooby, illegally, in 1607, and he was excommunicated in September 1607.

The church at Headon was a puritan stronghold for a generation. (Author)

He certainly knew Smyth (and may even have been in his congregation briefly), Bernard and Brewster; he had been married by Hancock at Scrooby in 1593 to Jane Wastneys, from the main family in Headon, but there was a legal dispute about the lack of banns and Jane's having previously been married to William Riggs. Thomas and Edward Southworth – possibly relatives, although this is disputed – joined the Robinson congregation in Leiden and Edward's widow became Robinson's second wife.

Henry Gray, removed from Bawtry, was excommunicated in 1606 for 'pretending' to be curate at Headon. In 1620 Hancock was fined '6d for riot', at a special sessions in Laneham to try twenty-six people indicted for riotous assault. The parish had both a rector and a vicar, the former having no responsibility for the souls of the parish – so in the early 1800s the rector was getting £18 a year for doing nothing. The Wastneys found Hancock a better living at Todwick in 1623.

There was an illegal Baptist 'conventicle' here in 1669 and Headon later became a home for Quakers; George Wheldale had goods of £20 seized for holding Quaker meetings at his house, having been informed on by John Reynor of Drayton.

Hibaldstow:

Hygbald (or Hibald) was a seventh century Northumbrian missionary, presumed to have given his name to this village and to have become Abbot of Bardney. He is also known for the survival of a penitential prayer in which he starts by describing himself as 'a miserable and unworthy homunculus' and then calls for forgiveness addressing the Father, the Son and the Spirit. It has been noted that 'he addresses the Son and the Spirit in the same way'. His way of commenting on sins of thought, word and deed reflects Irish influence; Bede tells us that he went to Ireland to visit Ecgbehrt and had a prophetic vision of the death of Chad.

Hygbald was buried at Hibaldstow in about 690 and a shrine, which became a place of pilgrimage, was erected. This survived until the Reformation when it was destroyed and the saint's remains presumed lost. However, in the mid-1860s work began on rebuilding the church and a Saxon stone coffin containing the remains of a man and a crozier was discovered beneath the altar.

John Wesley visited in June 1742 as he had a brother and sister living here; he walked from Epworth.

The Methodist preacher on the Gainsborough Circuit appointed in 1799 was

Joseph Pescod, extracts of whose diary have survived. He tells an interesting story about the chapel here:

> Dec. 30. I went to Hibbiston [Hibaldstow]. The man who built the Chapel was impelled thereto by a Dream wherein the spot of ground was shewed to him. He bought it and built ye Chapel. I had many attentive hearers.

During the 1800s the village suffered the fragmentation of Methodism that we have seen elsewhere. A new Wesleyan Methodist chapel was built in 1814, a Primitive Methodist one in 1841 and a Free Methodist one in 1865; this meant there were seats for six hundred nonconformists in a village of only seven hundred and fifty-four people. No wonder the vicar felt he needed to build a 'tin tabernacle'.

Horkstow:

A Roman mosaic which some have suggested has Christian elements to its design was found at Horkstow in 1796. The mosaic was from a Roman villa and, it has been suggested, this belonged to a former Roman soldier: the church at Horkstow is dedicated to St Martin, a Roman soldier martyred for refusing to kill German Christians in 297AD.

Kirton in Lindsey:

The name of this small market town indicates it had a church from an early date and this may have been one of the 'episcopal minsters' later held by the first Norman Bishop of Lincoln, Remigius. The future Queen Katherine Parr briefly lived here during her first marriage.

The grammar school founded in 1577 is linked to the Brocklesby and Wray family, and Sir Christopher Wray provided for scholars of the school to go to Magdalene College, Cambridge. Few ever did, but one was Henry Waterland, son of the rector of Broughton, in 1656. Moses Mell was removed as vicar in 1662 and was, according to one historian, a Baptist.

One history refers to the Baptist congregation at Kirton as an 'ancient' one, dating back to at least the 1650s , and to have been 'zealous', despite persecution. The leader, John Kelsey, was imprisoned in Lincoln in 1660, and by 1663 had been moved to Nottingham Gaol where he seems to have remained until 1687, though not necessarily continuously. During much of this time he corresponded – largely in rhyme – with Aaron Jeffery at Gamston. In 1672 the Declaration of Indulgences permitted the licensing of houses for Baptists and others, causing consternation for Lincoln's Bishop Fuller who thought 'all the licensed persons grow insolent and increase strangely'; but the Declaration was revoked in 1673. Kirton was one of the first Lincolnshire churches to join the Baptist New Connexion and its evangelistic outlook was shown in setting up an 'outstation' in the industrial hamlet at Cleatham in 1879.

John Wesley preached here in 1780. He spoke to a 'very large and serious congregation' but saw one who was resistant, as he thought, because he kept his hat on during prayer. Wesley could not resist telling a story about the Governor of Jamaica, who apparently took off his hat to a passing black man; when the latter expressed surprise, the governor said (according to Wesley), 'Sir, I should be ashamed if a negro had more good manners than the Governor of Jamaica'. Perhaps, but a hundred and fifty years before, keeping your hat on would have been the mark of a Puritan.

Wesley was not keen on women preaching and female evangelists such as Ann Carr of Market Rasen found it difficult to be accepted in the Wesleyans. One of her first public sermons was preached at Kirton in 1820 when 'two souls were made happy and one backslider restored'. Carr found a more comfortable place with the Primitive Methodists and had great success in Nottingham and Leeds thereafter.

Kneesall:

We tend to think of the parish system as 'fixed' for centuries, but in 1403 the parishioners here were so 'intermingled' with Boughton that it was decided to join the two parishes, Boughton not producing enough to support its rector; Boughton became a 'chapelry' of Kneesall, until 1535, and permanently separated in 1866. It was a village noted for Puritans. Two clergymen were ejected in 1662 as Charles II tightened his control of the Church of England. In the late 1600s the leaders of the Baptist conventicle here were two former Anglican clergymen: Thomas Casse, ejected from St. Mary Magdalene, Fleet Street, London, and John Jackson, the ejected minister from Bleasby, who kept a school in the village and managed to preach twice on Sundays. In 1669 both Baptists and Quakers were holding meetings in the village, their total number coming to more than forty; Quakers were still meeting in 1764. In 1826 the General Baptists built a chapel in Boughton, with open-air baptisms at Whitewater Bridge in the 1830s.

Littleborough:

In 627 (or possibly 628) King Edwin, his nobles, and large numbers of people were baptised at York by Paulinus. This conversion was hugely significant because there was no Christian king in 'England' outside of the Kent enclave.

The ancient church at Littleborough incorporates fragments of Roman building and stands at the birthplace of Christianity in our region. (Author)

Edwin later persuaded the King of the East Angles to convert too.

After extensive missionary activity in the North, Paulinus – 'venerable and awe-inspiring' – came south as Edwin also held title to the kingdom of Lindsey. Lindsey, the kingdom of the Lindissi, probably also included Axholme and the modern Nottinghamshire district of Bassetlaw, which was a 'regio' of this little kingdom. That day, in the presence of Edwin and the deacon James, thousands were said to have been baptised in the River Trent at noon – 'a great multitude' including the governor of Lincoln.

This event, marking the true start to Christianity in this region, occurred at 'Tiovulfingacester,' which is most logically Littleborough where the Roman Road from Lincoln crossed the Trent, and we know the road was still an attraction since King Harold came this way in 1066.

Another attempt to portray Paulinus, here as a blond youth in Anglo-Catholic vestments (Author)

- *We may assume the baptisms took place by the Roman causeway across the Trent at the 'bottom' of the village; so Christianity began here.*

- *The tiny church is a fascinating survival, incorporating Roman brickwork*

The ferry at Littleborough; the Roman ford where the baptisms occurred was upstream to the left. (Picture the Past, Notts CC)

Mansfield:

This town was at the centre of radical Christianity from about 1570 to 1690. In 1574 two Mansfield men were brought before the Archdeacon for nonconformity and dismissed his labelling of them: 'Master Archdeacon knoweth no more what a Puritan is than his ould horse'. In 1582 Robert Dickons, a Leicestershire youth apprenticed in Mansfield, claimed that he was 'Elijah' (or 'Elias) as an angel had called him so in visions, 'sent from God to perfect some defects in the prophecy of Malachi'; he was attacked in a sermon by Henry Smith, the best preacher of his generation, and apparently 'renounced his blasphemies'.

John Darrell (c1562-c1607 or after) was born here and first became well-known in 1586 when he helped with a Derbyshire woman who was demon-possessed. He was called in by Isabel Foljambe (see Glentworth etc), who clearly knew of his abilities. It was doubly controversial, because most Protestants disapproved of supernatural talk as being Catholic superstition. After some effort the woman was apparently cured but Darrell then tried to bring a case of witchcraft against another woman, causing some opposition from Isabel Foljambe's husband. Darrell moved to Leicestershire (where Isabel had connections); he was involved in further exorcisms in 1596 and 1597, then became embroiled in another in Nottingham later that year.

This brought the conservative forces in the Church of England down upon him, and he was convicted of fraud though allowed to return quietly to Nottinghamshire. Darrell inspired a change in the Church's canon law so that exorcism could not be practised without authority.

He certainly came across the various 'Pilgrim' leaders at that time, but opposed separation from the Church.

Richard Rothwell was a Lancashire firebrand who was brought to Mansfield in 1621 by the same Isabel (by this stage remarried and retitled Lady Darcy), who had previously used him to evangelise parts of County Durham.

An extract from the register of Quakers and Dissenters kept at Mansfield in the early 1700s. (Picture the Past, Nottinghamshire County Council)

He was a firebrand nonconformist and was preacher at a town where the vicar was a conformist, yet he had complete freedom to preach there and in other churches thereabouts.

Lady Darcy wanted a good Puritan preacher as Mansfield's incumbent clergyman was a drunkard. Rothwell famously got involved with another demoniac case, which he resolved in characteristically robust fashion. In his own last months, Rothwell seems to have occasionally lost his reason.

The face of a Quaker: Mary Turner of Mansfield, c.1800. (Picture the Past, Mansfield Museum & Art Gallery)

On his death bed, he recited a psalm and his last words were 'Blessed is he that hath not bowed the knee to Baal'.

George Fox (1624-91), the Quaker leader, lived for a time in Chesterfield Road, currently the site of St Philip Neri's Catholic Church, where he was a bootmaker. The turning point in Fox's life, as he later recalled, came some time in 1647 when in Mansfield he heard a voice saying 'There is one, even Jesus Christ, that can speak to thy Condition.' From then on Fox proclaimed the present accessibility of God who 'was now come to teach his People himself.' There was no need to rely on human teachers for even the scriptures were less authoritative than one's inward guide. Whilst walking past the church, he heard God tell him 'that which people trample on must be thy food'.

He held meetings, including one in 1648 where 'the Lord's power was so great that the house seemed to be shaken'.

Fox recounts a number of experiences here, including in 1648 when 'one of the most wicked men in the country' was convicted of sin and converted.

Old houses
Chesterfield R⁴   A.S.BUXTON.

The house where Fox lived in Mansfield has sadly been demolished and a Catholic 'steeplehouse' built on the site - he would not have approved! (Mansfield Museum & Art Gallery)

Two with less impact! Firstly, William Chappell (1582-1649) was born in Laxton but went to school in Mansfield, then to Christ's College where he was briefly tutor to John Milton. Starting as a Puritan, his theology became more Arminian and this made him a favourite of Archbishop Laud. After a controversial career at Trinity College and as a bishop in Ireland, he was an outcast in the 1640s and retired to Bilsthorpe where there is a memorial to him and to his brother, who held the living of Mansfield Woodhouse. Richard Sterne of Mansfield was educated in the town and became Archbishop of York in 1664. As a Laudian and Royalist he had a difficult 1640s but after the Restoration rose rapidly. However, he attracted much negative comment!

The layout of the Stockwell Gate Baptist church in Mansfield reflected the central purpose of preaching the word. (Picture the Past, Nottinghamshire County Council)

For political reasons Mansfield was attractive to nonconformists. 'Rejected' ministers like John Billingsley, Matthew Sylvester, Joseph Truman (see Cromwell), William Reynolds and John Whitlock gathered here until the latter two left in 1686 to run the Presbyterian congregation in Nottingham. The next generation were also ordained here.

Later, Henry Clarke (1828-1907), born of humble origins in Mansfield, spent most of his life working for Christ in Jamaica. He was briefly educated at the grammar school before becoming a pupil teacher in Coningsby. His biographer concludes 'a distinctive, radical, devout voice which spoke on issues—and on behalf of people—neglected by Jamaica's élites'; he showed a genuine commitment to the poor and the abandoned, founding a Building Society to help provide them with homes, and was 'utterly fearless'.

- *Consult the excellent Quaker trail now published online, but start at the Catholic Church in Chesterfield Road - Fox's home.*

- *St Peter and St Paul's Church is generally assumed to be where, walking by, Fox had his first significant revelation.*

Mansfield Woodhouse:

Dr Ralph Snoden of Mansfield Woodhouse was a persecutor of non-conformists; his third son, Robert, was able to bring healing to a woman tormented by a spirit here in 1649.

George Fox, the Quaker leader, went to the parish church (or 'steeple house' as he would call it) to 'admonish' its priest and congregation, but they beat him with sticks and – he says – Bibles. Then they put him in the stocks, presumably in the market place, and then drove him out of town. In 1658 two Quaker women were put in the stocks for using words 'displeasing' to the priest.

A Baptist church started at Mansfield in 1815 when Robert Smith baptised five people in the river at Mansfield Woodhouse in front of a crowd of two thousand; one who 'had resolved to turn the solemn service with ridicule' was overcome by the Holy Spirit.

Over the centuries the church here has survived fire, earthquake, vandalism and subsidence – quite a triumph!

An old print reputedly shows Fox in the stocks at Mansfield Woodhouse, accompanied by an unwelcome drunk it would appear!

The tranquil modern setting of Mansfield Woodhouse church belies its often turbulent past! (Author)

Marnham:

This small Trentside village had a succession of radical priests, including Richard Clyfton, the leader of the 'Brewster congregation' in 1586. In 1604 Henry Aldred and John Herring seem to have begun a dispute over the living, which resulted in court appearances at Retford and Newark for several clergymen – including also John Smyth. Herring lost and went to Basford, close to where Thomas Helwys lived; both men preached without a licence at Greasley.

In 1608 Mr Edwards, clerk, was preaching there without a licence, and by 1619 Marnham had Robert Hargreaves, also without a licence, who was cited for not using the sign of the cross in baptism, not using a ring in a wedding, nor wearing a surplice. By 1621 Hargreaves had been ordained priest and the following year was reportedly vicar of Kneesall. Hargreaves and Ash, the vicar of Marnham, were cited for holding 'private religious exercises' at Ash's vicarage.

The rather remote church at Marnham became, like Headon, a centre of puritan activity for a generation. (Author)

This was the age of the 'gentleman parson', but perhaps few were as extraordinary as Edmund Cartwright, who was born at Marnham in 1743. An academic and a poet, he found enough time between his duties as a clergyman to study medicine as well, despite holding benefices in four places. From 1771 to 1779 he was also vicar of his birthplace village. In 1784 he became interested in the mechanisation of weaving and patented a powered loom the following year. However, Cartwright was not a businessman, and attempts to set up his own factories in Doncaster and Retford failed whilst other entrepreneurs pirated his designs. Eventually he was rewarded by a Parliamentary grant of £10,000 in 1809. His brothers took a different path – one became a radical politician and another an explorer – whilst his daughter Elizabeth became the famous writer Mrs Markham (see Fledborough).

Mattersey:

The Gilbertine house at Mattersey was founded in about 1185. A Gilbertine house, it was visited by Leigh and Layton in 1536, who found one of the canons to be 'incontinent'. It was surrendered in 1538.

William Pontus was a rather belligerent churchwarden here before joining Robinson in the Netherlands and going to New England in 1630.

The Rev William Aspinwall of Mattersey was indicted at Retford in 1661 for not reading the Book of Common Prayer; he became a farmer at Thurnscoe and later a Presbyterian or Congregational minister in Lancashire. He may have been one of those ordained 'unofficially' at Clayworth with John Cromwell.

Now the village is best known as the national headquarters and training centre (since 1973) of the Assemblies of God, a Pentecostal denomination set up in 1924 in this country. Students come from all over the world to train here, and the college's influence is truly international. David Prakasam (1974-76) came from India and has since planted some six hundred and fifty churches in eighteen provinces there, in Nepal and in Sri Lanka, and is still heavily involved in Medical Camps, providing financial aid for families in hardship, Leper Rehabilitation, Widow Care Homes and looking after children in Orphan Care homes. Mark Ritchie, who graduated in 1992, has planted twenty churches in the Philippines.

Messingham:

This village was central to intense activity by the Primitive Methodists, starting with William Braithwaite's preaching in 1818. Thomas Kendall, the carrier, pulled up near the tree (known as the 'Cross Tree') where the preacher was standing in the main street:

'Conviction for sin seized him while he listened, and it was of so powerful a nature that he often declared his hair rose up upon his head and displaced his hat...'

The Primitive Methodists built a simple chapel in Messingham but they soon diverted their energies and funds into building striking but unnecessary edifices. (Author's collection)

The village was 'the favoured spot' in the revival of 1830. Hundreds came there, so that the lanes were 'vocal with the song of praise'.

- *The tree is gone, but there is still a junction with Cross Tree Lane to mark the spot.*

Primitive Methodists held their revivalist meetings in the centre of Messingham, by the tree indicated here. Now you would be arrested for blocking the road! (Author's collection)

MESSINGHAM, SHOWING THE TREE UNDER WHICH THE SERVICE WAS HELD.

Misterton:

This was an 'ancient' Baptist community, perhaps from 1676. Claims that this was the first place where Particular (Calvinist) and General (Arminian) Baptists were united seem based on a new chapel opening in 1761 that served both. For years in the early 1800s the church was served by Mr Skidmore of Retford, who walked the twelve miles every Sunday, despite being blind. 'He tramped some twenty thousand miles to minister to only half-a-dozen. After his day there was a great revival there. He was totally blind. His wife led him every step of the way'. The General Baptists were extinct by 1833 as they had all died, but Fogg of Retford formed a new church and several were baptised in 1848; Mr Hurt was the minister c1847-51. In 1851 the General Baptists held a mission meeting which Mr Fogg, of Retford, wrote a report on:

'This appears a barren spot, and unfruitful soil, yet we called to remembrance that from this place men have been raised up that were valiant for the truth. Our brother who labours there is exceedingly discouraged, and sows in tears'.

John Wesley preached at Misterton seventeen times from 1749. The chapel of 1756 was one of the earliest built. Wesley crossed the marshy Haxey Carr from Axholme. In 1757 he told of a Stockwith woman who dreamed of drowning whilst crossing – and then, deciding to travel anyway, fell off her horse into a ditch that was barely a yard deep and drowned because no-one thought to help her out. He preached to a very large congregation at Misterton, disrupted only by the Baptist minister; Wesley felt tired, so gave up arguing with him and left.

In 1761 he found a 'lifeless, money-getting people', despite the opening of a chapel.

In 1766 he paid a 'pastoral visit' to a young woman afflicted by melancholy: 'we were quickly convinced where her disorder came…this kind goeth not out but by prayer and fasting'. In 1774 Jeremiah Brettell was appointed to the Epworth circuit and revival broke out in Misterton when Thomas Corbett preached: Brettell recalled that 'a divine power descended upon the whole assembly…many were in tears'. Later Corbett, whilst riding, had an impression 'This moment my father is dying,' which proved to be the case.

Wesley found 'the work of God exceedingly decayed' in 1790, although he still had to preach under a tree as 'the house' was too small to accommodate everyone. On one occasion his arrival was disrupted by floodwater

John Wesley was a frequent visitor to Misterton where Methodism was strong for generations. (Author's collection)

and, on the way back, his mare banged into a gate and left the great preacher behind, flat on his back.

Methodism remained strong, the chapel was rebuilt in 1826 and there were 'revivals' in 1835 and 1853. After a week of prayer and visiting homes, the Misterton Methodists saw 'signs and wonders wrought' whilst forty to fifty souls were saved in a week. In 1835 the village had a church, chapels for both Calvinistic and Wesleyan Methodists, plus Baptist and Roman Catholic chapels. Quite a choice!

Joseph Tindall (1807-1861) was born at Gringley and grew up at Misterton, which he called 'a place of darkness', from 1809. After a youth spent 'in the pleasures of sin' he was converted and became a famous Wesleyan missionary in South Africa and Namibia from 1835, where his work was much aided when he offered 'incessant prayer for rain' and there was 'an abundance of rain'. His son also became a missionary.

Morton:

This was one of the most neglected parishes in England. A vicar was appointed in 1568 who was dead by 1614, and no other until 1662. Probably this was because the benefice paid badly, but during the Civil War period William Quipp 'filled in' – saying his own benefice had no church or people (possibly this was Sudbrooke), so he had been invited by the people of Morton (and Torksey) to help them. He was perhaps the son of John Quipp, the vicar of Littleborough, and the grandson of John Quippe of Sturton, the priest to Smyth and Robinson. Quipp was removed from Morton in 1662, but got into further trouble in 1672-3 and 1679. He spent a time in prison and was fined £13. He may have been the same man who was licensed as preacher at Kettlethorpe in 1684.

Muskham, North:

This was the birthplace of possibly Nottinghamshire's worst missionary – George Vason (1772-1838), although he labelled it 'an obscure village'. After a sinful youth, Vason was converted and in 1797 was sent by the London Missionary Society to Tahiti. In Tonga, after a problem with some mysterious British criminals, he 'went native'. Unfortunately, he went so native that he adopted all aspects of local life, including polygamy and tattoos. His short 'idyll' was interrupted by civil war and three British companions were killed. Vason later regretted that he 'disgraced my character as a Christian' and returned to live in Nottingham in 1801. There he was re-converted - although never again easy in talking about faith - and became the gaoler, marrying in

1804; you might think this would have counted as criminal bigamy, except perhaps Tongan marriages were not recognised by British law. Vason was a skilled linguist and is credited with having introduced the Tongan word 'taboo' into English.

Newton on Trent:

It was visited by John Wesley in July 1770 and on several other occasions including August 1781. In 1770 the heavy rain cleared up so he could preach outside, and he was pleased: 'an earnest congregation…a people more loving, more artless, or more athirst for God, I have seldom seen'. In May 1780 the congregation was 'large and genteel', whilst in 1790 only half of them could fit into the preaching house.

Hannah Hunt (nee Summers) was born here in 1812. In 1838 she married John Hunt (of Balderton and Swinderby) in the parish church and set off for life as a Wesleyan missionary in Fiji, having expected South Africa - a celebrated career ending only in his death, after which she returned to Newton. Helen and one of their daughters are buried at Newton.

Newton on Trent churchyard contains the graves of John Hunt's wife and daughter, the words 'born in Fiji' seeming striking even today. (Author)

- *Hunt was a great man, but stand in the church where they married and reflect on the step of faith Hannah took.*

- *The gravestones of Hannah and her daughter – 'born in Fiji' – can be found easily on the SE corner of the church.*

- *You can also visit the memorial chapel at Thorpe, where he was filled with the Spirit, rebuilt in 1909.*

Hunt looks focused and determined in this print published after his death. (Author's collection)

Ollerton, Old:

Ollerton was the home of the Markham family who, by the 1590s, had shown interest in Catholicism. Sir Griffin Markham was a Catholic and saw the accession of James I as an opportunity, although he was equally motivated by the desire to reclaim family lands. He hatched a misguided plot to kidnap the new King, imprison him in the Tower, and demand both freedom of religion and return of his lands. His twin brothers seem to have done their best to avoid being involved. It all went wrong, of course, and Markham was sentenced to death but, on the scaffold, this was commuted to exile for life. In or before 1595 he had married Anne, daughter of Peter Roos of Laxton. Her husband banished, Anne contracted a bigamous marriage with her manservant, James Sanford. This irregularity was soon common knowledge, and she was forced to perform penance at Paul's Cross in November 1617. Sir Griffin cannot really be seen as suffering for his faith, and few Catholics helped him.

Ollerton is most significant as the birthplace of Elizabeth Hooton, the famous Quaker preacher (see Skegby). She married a farmer and a son was baptised in 1633. Although her earliest children were christened here, she later became a Baptist and may even have preached as one although she seems to have been disappointed by their neglect. The Quakers saw no problem in women preaching. Between 1633 and 1636 she moved with her husband to Skegby, west of Mansfield. What followed was a brilliant career as a Quaker preacher and missionary.

The Baptists did not fade away totally. In the 1830-40 period baptisms were conducted in the pool at Wellow Green and Whitewater Bridge.

Owston Ferry:

The village is unusual in that the church is situated partly inside Kinaird (or Kinnard) Castle's bailey, conferring rights on the lord. By 1640 Owston was a nonconformist centre with a number of Baptists.

John Wesley preached here many times from 1742, perhaps around twenty times in all. According to W B Stonehouse, his usual place was under a tree at the west end. In June 1742 he received word that the minister had invited him to speak using the church, but was then refused, so he preached 'in another place.'

He used the ferry here to get to and from Gainsborough. In 1743 he nearly drowned while crossing the Trent on his way from Epworth to Grimsby. It was a stormy day and the ferrymen were hesitant to cross, and Wesley delayed an hour. Then he used a bit of persuasion with the result that 'if we would venture our lives, they would venture theirs'. They set out with six men, two women and three horses, with plenty watching. But in the middle, 'in an instant, the side of the boat was under water, and the horses and men rolling over one another. We expected the boat to sink at any moment, but I did not doubt of being able to swim ashore'.

Wesley seemed full of calm assurance. However, there is a trace of irony in his account, for next the boatmen recovered, the horses leapt overboard, and they came safely to shore - but Wesley did not move. In all the trouble, an iron crow bar had penetrated the laces of his boots, effectively pinning him down, so his confidence about swimming ashore was badly misplaced. His also noted that his brother had a similar escape on the Severn at almost the same time.

The 1837 Methodist chapel is a fine example of the type in a village that is important in Methodist history. (Author)

In 1744 Methodist preacher John Downes was arrested here. Later Elizabeth Dunting of Owston was a thirteen year-old girl who experienced a powerful religious conversion and then died of 'convulsions' in 1767; her story was widely used as an inspiration to others.

When Wesley preached in 1774 he noted that: 'One of my audience here was Mr. Pinder, a contemporary of mine at Oxford. But any that observed so feeble, decrepit an old man, tottering over the grave, would imagine there was a difference of forty rather than two years between us!"

In June 1786 he preached at Owston church and was cared for by Gervase Woodhouse, a member of a local family with Epworth connections and a JP; Woodhouse is also recorded as having been supportive of Methodist missionaries, even giving them food from his own house – though this may have been largely his wife's doing. Wesley knew Woodhouse's wife Elizabeth from the 1760s, and often wrote to her from 1764 to 1780. She was one of a number of women that the great preacher tended to be distracted by. Wesley preached there again in 1788 and afterwards visited Mr Pinder's derelict mansion.

The Methodist New Connexion was set up in 1798 by Alexander Kilham, who was living in Owston but went to Epworth for a revival meeting. A Primitive Methodist chapel was opened here in 1820 and closed in 1962. In an 1823 service, 'In the evening we both heard him (S. Bayley) preaching at the Ferry. After preaching there was a prayer meeting; our brother formed a penitent square, exhorting and entreating those penitents to come into it'. Many camp meetings were held on the nearby recreation field and at Scotter Hill across the Trent.

It has been claimed that the religious census of 1851 showed Owston as the 'most Methodist' place in Britain. In the 1870s the Methodist minister was Rev H Keet who, when his daughter died, wanted her buried with a gravestone recording him as 'Rev' Keet or as a 'Wesleyan Minister.' The vicar refused permission, claiming no dissenter could be titled 'Rev'; the case was discussed by the Archbishop, who supported Keet, and the Bishop, who supported his clergyman. However, this division was not so evident among the people, with many attending both church and chapel in the 1870s.

- *At the riverside reflect on Wesley's risky boat journey. It is a good place to consider the fragility of life – in Wesley's case he had at least two narrow escapes from death.*

- *Enjoy a visit to the surviving Methodist Chapel – it gives a taste of how powerful the Methodist revival must have been in this place.*

Oxton:

Almost on the margins of our region, but worth including because Sir Kenneth Grubb (1900-1980) was born here, the son of the evangelical rector, in 1900. He joined the Worldwide Evangelization Crusade and spent years exploring the upper Amazon and learning tribal languages. By 1927 he knew around twenty dialects and then moved to survey missionary work in South America. He became President of the Church Missionary Society and then a key influence on the formation of the World Council of Churches. The CMS had been founded following discussions between Charles Jerram, born in Blidworth with John Pugh – both Lincolnshire clergymen. Grubb also led the Christian Literature Crusade.

His older brother Norman (1895-1993) was born in Bournemouth before the family moved to Oxton in 1897. He also became an important missionary, was open about his faith during military service and was married to the daughter of the famous cricketer-turned-missionary, C T Studd, with whom he worked on the 'Heart of Africa Mission'. He had a significant impact in Zaire and in improving mission organisation. Violet Grubb, their sister, went to China in the 1920s to teach.

Sir Kenneth Grubb left Oxton to become a worldwide influence in the mission field. (World Council of Churches)

Retford, East and West:

Retford's dominant families (Denman, Hercy, Sloswicke) had Puritan leanings from 1550 which put them at the centre of the local networks of the 'godly'. William Denman (d.1587), a Cambridge graduate and the wealthy rector of Ordsall from 1550, temporarily lost his position under Mary I but when he became lord of the manor of West Retford in 1572 he was able to work alongside his mother's relatives the Hercys at Grove in appointing Puritan clergy, including his own brother Francis at West Retford; Sir John Hercy had been guardian to John Lassells, the Protestant martyr. William left a choice of his best books to

The 'day trip' was a key part of church life for generations - here Retford's Primitive Methodists set out for an unknown destination in 1906. (Picture the Past, Nottinghamshire County Council)

'Mr Clyfton', probably the later separatist leader John Denman's brother in law was Walter Travers, a Puritan of the highest influence.

Between 1590 and 1606 an evangelical 'clan' appointed Puritan clergy who, in turn, brought connections to other families such as the Wrays and Helwyses. East and West Retford, Ordsall and Babworth churches all were involved.

One of Denman's associates, George Turvin of East Retford, was in trouble for his Puritan leanings in 1592 and repeatedly for the next ten years. The Rector of West Retford from 1578-96 was Francis Denman, whose curate in 1591-2 was Thomas Hancock, the former curate from Scrooby; both were Puritans. Clearly some of the Retford Puritans attended Clyfton's services at Babworth and, after he was removed, thirteen Retford people got into trouble in May 1605 for 'gadding' to Sturton to listen to John Robinson preach – including local notables John Denman, John Sloswicke and Robert Parnell. In 1606 Anne Denman disrupted a service at Babworth, taken by a conforming Turvin, due to his use of rituals.

Puritans who moved to the Netherlands from 1608 included the Bannister family from here, Dorothy Pettinger, John Williams and James Hurst. But the rebellious tradition continued in East Retford, where Rev. John Watt was in trouble in 1623 for not following the Prayer Book, not meeting corpses at the church stile and, more significantly, refusing to wear the surplice and allowing 'strange' ministers to preach.

James Parnell, the first 'Quaker martyr', was christened in East Retford on 6 September 1636, the son of churchwarden Thomas Parnell. At the age of fifteen, he began searching for spiritual sustenance after finding little provided by the churches of his own town. Parnell's grammar school education was even worse:

> 'I was sent unto the schools of humane learning for to learn human wisdom, for which the schools are profitable, but for the attaining of heavenly wisdom and knowledge they are as far unprofitable, and many books that are there read are much for the corrupting of youth and the nourishment of the wild, profane nature which then ruled me'.

A later biographer wrote:

> 'His wicked natural propensities were nourished by the education he received; so that, whilst at school, and also after leaving it, the same depravity of heart remained, and he grew in sin, and continued to follow the sinful vanities of the world'.

Parnell sought a more powerful spiritual experience and joined up with a 'Seeker' community at Balby. He had 'visitations of heavenly light', forsook his sinful but popular lifestyle and became some cause of local amazement, so he was sometimes mocked in the streets. Remarkably, he walked to Carlisle and back to visit the Quaker leader, George Fox, who was in prison there.

Parnell became a Quaker preacher known as the 'Quaking Boy', antagonising the authorities in Cambridge and Essex, and founding new churches in Essex. In Colchester he was viciously attacked 'by a blind zealot who struck him a violent Blow with a great Staff, saying, "There, take that for Christ's Sake"'. He was arrested after disrupting a service at Coggeshall and died in Colchester Castle dungeons in 1656, the first Quaker 'martyr.'

One of Retford's architectural highlights is the Trinity Hospital, founded in 1665 from a bequest by John Darrell, a relative of the Denmans.

Colchester has a lively memorial marking the imprisonment and death of James Parnell, but Retford has nothing as yet.

Richard Brownlow's will left land in West Retford in 1691 to allow the preachers who had used this site to continue to do so. It was clear that the Retford Baptists were already meeting in Brownlow's 'newest built' house before he wrote the will. There has been a Baptist congregation in Retford ever since and at times it has been a national centre for the denomination; in 1789 the Baptist New Connexion met at Retford and agreed to collect all the best hymns they could. This resulted in *Hymns and Spiritual Songs* (1793), containing over six hundred, although it was widely known as *Dan Taylor's Hymns*.

Samuel Wright, who spent the first years of his life in Retford, grew up to become one of the most celebrated nonconformist preachers of his day.

It is difficult to establish his early life with certainty, but it is likely that both his father and grandfather were nonconformist preachers too. Once in London, he was a great success despite his meeting house being wrecked in a riot in 1710; a big new meeting house was opened in 1732. His preaching was said to be so striking that even Anglican bishops came to hear him and he published more than forty books, including a famous treatise on being born again.

Wesley's journal only records one sermon preached in Retford, so the start of Methodism in the town is generally attributed to a humble Scotsman widely known as 'Johnny Mack'. John McFarland (there are several spellings!) arrived in 1776, became a boatman on the canal and later a rather unsuccessful shopkeeper. He ended his life in the workhouse having refused a place in Trinity Hospital, which he thought too much like supping with the Devil - such was his suspicion of anything Anglican!

When Wesley visited Retford in 1779 John Willey led a mob intent on disrupting the preaching in the Market Place, but Johnny Mack organised his own group to 'manage' proceedings. Only one man managed to throw an egg – which hit his own sister, who rewarded him with a torrent of abuse!

With Johnny's help, the Methodists managed to open a chapel on what is now Spa Road, just off Carolgate. This had two separate entrances and railings down the middle so that the two genders could not sit together! As Johnny Mack got older and deafer the Methodist chapel got bigger, so he was given special permission to sit on the pulpit steps to hear the sermon. In 1786 Wesley preached in an orchard behind 29 Bridgegate on the text ' I saw the dead, small and great, stand before God'– the Civic Society has put a plaque up to commemorate this.

The Methodist Rev William Naylor started work in Retford in 1802 at the tender age of twenty with no transport until his parents gave him a pony. He was meant to get paid £12 a year in four instalments, but the money had run out before he got his first payment! One night the pony 'disappeared' from his lodgings and his landlady told Naylor he would need to walk to Tuxford, which he accepted with good humour; this impressed her so much, she later became a Methodist. Naylor got his pony back, but its tail had been shaved, the mane shorn and its flanks oddly marked. The story was told that this happened as he had refused to pay the road toll - perhaps understandable!

Naylor left Retford for the Leeds area where he helped start the Wesleyan Missionary Society in 1813, but his active circuit ministry lasted until 1862 and he gave a sermon at the anniversary of the Society in 1863, the last survivor of its founders; at the time of his death in 1868, Naylor was the oldest minister in the Connexion. He was clearly well known to James and Mary Wallis who led the first successful mission amongst the New Zealand Maoris; when chief Te Awaitaia was converted in 1836 he took a new 'Christian' name Wiremu Neera, which was the closest pronunciation of 'William Naylor.' Naylor also liked to do a bit of writing and entered into the 'pamphlet wars' mode of operation; one can only guess the subject of his 1815 effort entitled *'Report of the Speeches delivered at an Extraordinary Congress, convened by His Satanic Majesty, for the purpose of taking into consideration the propriety of presenting James Douglas with a Vote of Thanks for his late attempts, in two pamphlets, to render Methodism contemptible, and Devilism respectable'.* Grove Street chapel was built in 1879, showing the influence and popularity that Methodism had attained by this time.

George Rex and his wife were influential nonconformists in both Retford and Gainsborough. (Author's collection)

Later the town gained a variety of other groups including the Primitive Methodists who were nicknamed 'ranters' and took over an old theatre in Carolgate; the group held 'camp meetings' on Spa Common in 1869.

Sarah 'Lizzie' Harrison, (d. 1900), was a Retford housewife born in Leeds, who was widowed after nearly twenty years. An old friend was Jane Hercus, a schoolteacher, who had lodged with Lizzie's family in Leeds and then married the 'flamboyant' Rev. James Chalmers (1841-1901), a Scot; Chalmers went with the London Missionary Society to the South Seas in 1865 with his new wife – and got shipwrecked on the way! He believed missionaries should live and eat in the native lifestyle and that the success of the Church depended on developing an indigenous leadership. He became 'a bearded frontier evangelist'. Chalmers transferred to New Guinea in 1871 where he displayed phenomenal energy, but where his wife, after much service and suffering, died in 1879.

It would seem the original plan had been for Lizzie to join them on mission but instead she married Harrison, 'a very excellent Christian gentleman'. She appeared in the Census for 1881 as 'house keeper'.

The house in Alma Road, Retford, whose comforts Lizzie Harrison left behind for a new life as a missionary in Papua New Guinea. (Author)

Chalmers was in Papua New Guinea in 1881 when ten teachers, mostly native to the region, were killed and eaten by cannibals. The British sent a flotilla of gunboats to catch the perpetrators and kill them; Chalmers told a correspondent from The Times that he disclaimed, 'after years of work, ever having made a single convert to Christianity in New Guinea. All he hopes is that the germs of civilisation planted in the present generation may someday render future ones capable of receiving the teaching of the Gospel'. Lizzie and Chalmers had lost touch but she contacted him after he published his first book.

In 1886 Chalmers revisited Britain, breaking his journey to Scotland with the Harrisons. Harrison caught flu and, while Chalmers was away, he died. Chalmers – now a substantial celebrity – came back to help and soon an 'engagement' had been made.

James Chalmers, who found new love in Retford, and lost his new wife annd his own life in Papua New Guinea. (Author's collection)

Lizzie agreed to share his work and its dangers, so the year following sailed to meet Chalmers in Australia, where they were married in October 1888 at Cooktown. They travelled on a steamer with the famous author of *Treasure Island*, Robert Louis Stevenson.

Lizzie entered fully into the duties and privations of missionary life at Toaripi in New Guinea; she found the hard life and loneliness – Chalmers was often away – difficult. She had been 'used to all the comforts of a lovely English home', but had to endure Saguane, which even another missionary thought 'a dreadful place'. Lizzie faced fever and 'watched the destruction of all that she treasured from an English home'.

> 'At night bats fly in between the walls and roof. Ants and mosquitos also abound. If you look down on the mats and floors you perceive they are covered with life; even this paper is continually covered with tiny, moving things, which I blow off......There are about 3000 wild savages here, fine, handsome men, got up in truly savage style. I do believe I would rather face a crowd of them than the insects in the house.'

She had no close friends of her own culture. 'If I ever stop to think, I feel as if I can't live another day in this loneliness' she told a rare visitor. In 1891 Lizzie nearly died from recurring malaria and in 1892 Chalmers sent her to recover in England.

As Superintendent of many stations, Chalmers went on long journeys, while Lizzie carried on the work at the home stations. In 1894-5 they paid another visit to England, and Chalmers preached a 'farewell sermon' at the Congregational Church in Retford, saying 'I say goodbye to you, Christian friends...we shall never meet again...'. They returned to their work, and in 1900 Lizzie, wearied by the treacherous climate, died on board the mission ship. Chalmers wrote:

> 'She was a good, true, loving wife, a faithful, earnest follower of Christ, always blithe and hearty, and seldom looked on life's dark side ...For fourteen weeks she was ill, but steadily growing in Christ ... She was thankful for her long illness, notwithstanding the great suffering, as it gave her time to understand better, to get a clearer view and a stronger faith. Often she could be heard in praise, saying, "Peace, perfect peace!" "In my Father's house are many mansions." "Jesus is near, very near"'.

On 8 April 1901 – Easter Sunday – on an expedition to Goaribari Island with the Rev Oliver Tompkins, Chalmers and his party of twelve were captured, killed, beheaded and eaten by cannibals.

Although Lizzie's old church is now the site of a supermarket, Retford has several new churches – Catholic, Methodist and Baptists have all built in the last seventy-five years.

The rather austere Congregational church in Retford was replaced by a supermarket; it was the last place in Britain that James Chalmers preached. (Picture the Past, Nottinghamshire County Council)

It has a twenty-first century Baptist church rebuilt on its original 1691 site. Before the old one was demolished, a prophecy was given that the church would be a well from which others could come and be refreshed and so it was renamed 'The Well'. When the Victorian edifice was knocked down an ancient well was found – right outside the new front door. Possibly this was the well which provided the water for baptisms centuries ago, but it was a fitting discovery.

- *Adjacent to St Swithun's church is a dental practice, built on the site of Parnell's school. A good place to reflect on his journey and sacrifice.*

- *Chalmers preached his farewell sermon at where Aldi's supermarket is now; Lizzie's house was 42 Alma Road.*

- *Take a short walk from the bridge in Bridgegate (by the AoG church), passing the sign indicating the site of Wesley's sermon and noting the brown paint on the Trinity Hospital estate's buildings, to the old Denman church of West Retford. A few more yards takes you to the well outside the Baptist church, and then a little further to the Trinity Hospital almshouses.*

Sandtoft:

Sandtoft was the main base for the Dutch who came to drain the Carrs; Dutch, French or Walloon Protestant refugees (Huguenots) arrived in 1628 and 1635. Vermuyden, the engineer, promised a church would be built and a minister employed. In 1637 the Dutch and the Walloons complained that they still had no church and had been meeting at Crowtrees. By 1639 there was a chapel at Sandtoft with alternate services in Dutch and French; Peter Brontemps was the first pastor. In 1642 Jean Despagne was the French pastor; he was an influential reformed theologian.

The chapel was attacked by four hundred rioters in 1650-1, stirred up by radical republicans George Stovin and perhaps John Lilburne, but also a local solicitor Daniel Noddell. It was defaced, carrion buried beneath the altar, and the seats taken away. Lilburne used the church as a barn and lodged his servants in the minister's house, having destroyed much of Sandtoft. Lilburne later blamed the trouble on 'the multitude (who) did foolishly throw down many poor houses', though local people made clear they were aggrieved at their treatment by the drainage engineers. Stovin died in Lincoln Castle after the Restoration, having been arrested for attending an illegal place of worship.

By the 1680s few remained and they could barely support a minister; there is no record after 1685. By 1686 the locals had pulled down the Dutch church's fences and were grazing their cattle in its graveyard. Almost the only thing that survived was the French edition of the Geneva Bible, which was kept by a local family, whilst an old font at Crowle possibly came from here. There seems also to have been a French congregation in Thorne in the 1650s.

In 1697 Nathaniel Reading's house was burnt down the day after it had been completed; this obviously informed suspicions that Epworth Rectory suffered the same fate.

- *Sandtoft is now better known for its transport museum but it is a lonely place and Crow Trees, just to the NW, even lonelier. It is a good place to reflect on how Christian refugees have not always been well treated by other 'Christians' although the economic context at Sandtoft was complex.*

Saundby:

To access Saundby church you have to go through a farmyard, but it is well worth the effort as this is the the only church apart from Bilborough with a memorial connected to the Helwys family (see Askham), who held the manor

Saundby church was one of the 'home churches' of the Helwys family. (Author)

here amidst their other properties. Dating from 1599, and most likely erected by Sir Gervase Helwys (Elwes), who was executed on Tower Hill in 1615, it records that 'This is a work of piety, not of pride, and the work of deep affection, for in their own lifetime they taught me how I ought to honour them indeed'.

Helwys seems to have lived in Gainsborough from 1595 into the early 1600s but is also described as 'of Worlaby' and was influential in Lincolnshire; in 1605 he was able to appoint George Turvin as Clyfton's replacement at Babworth, and in 1613 was himself appointed Lieutenant of the Tower - but he was dragged into the scandal over the death of prisoner Sir Thomas Overbury, for which he was hung on Tower Hill in 1615. His death achieved great attention for he died repentant and expressing confidence in his salvation - indicating a Calvinist of Puritan leanings.

We may also speculate that Thomas Helwys, his nephew, must often have stayed here in 1606-8 if he met with John Smyth and the Gainsborough congregation with any frequency, for his own home was thirty miles away at Broxtowe. Saundby was - with Gainsborough - one of the livings that John Smyth thought tempted Richard Bernard to stay within the Church of England, but he never received either.

A contemporary print of Sir Gervase Helwys, who perhaps sought power and wealth with national responsibility but found only ignominy and disaster.

Saundby continued to be a Puritan enclave and its curate in the 1630s was Ephraim Tuke, one of the large clerical family that held livings in Lincolnshire and Nottinghamshire. In 1662 Joseph Rock was 'silenced' but was provided with a place by the landowner, John Disney.

Scotter:

There were perhaps Baptists here by the 1630s and in 1672 Thomas Williamson had a licence to preach.

John Wesley himself preached in Scotter many times from 1764 usually, as in 1774, in 'an open place':

> 'I preached, about nine, at Scotter, a town six or seven miles east of Epworth, where a sudden flame is broken out, many being convinced of sin almost at once, and many justified. But there were many adversaries stirred up by a bad man who told them, "There is no law for Methodists." Hence continual riots followed; till, after a while, an upright magistrate took the cause in hand and so managed both the rioters and him who set them at work that they have been quiet as lambs ever since'.

The magistrate was Sir Neville Hickman. In 1779 Wesley noted that 'the people walk "in the fear of the Lord and the comfort of the Holy Ghost."' In 1780 he preached to 'a lovely, simple-hearted people' and lastly in 1788 when he concluded 'I found it good to be there'. It seems to have been one of his favourite places.

Scotter was a centre for the Primitive Methodists and had a substantial chapel. (Author's collection)

The churchyard at Scotter, where George Shadford began his spiritual journey. (Author)

Scotter is of significance to American Methodists as the birthplace of George Shadford in 1739. Shadford was a difficult child who was cruel to animals and disobeyed the Sabbath but at around sixteen he experienced a re-awakening of faith. If you spend time in the churchyard of Scotter you can share the experience of the young Shadford, who came here to pray for several hours at a time. However, lacking Christian friends and with a love of sport and 'profane books', he lost his spiritual path.

Several years later he was with the militia in Gainsborough when he went to hear a Methodist preacher because some pretty girls were going. The girls were soon forgotten as Shadford was struck by the preacher's extempore prayer and preaching: 'I received more light from that single sermon than from all that I ever heard in my life before'.

Shadford became a Methodist preacher, then went to America in 1773. His greatest successes came in Virginia 1775-6 on the Brunswick Circuit, after he changed his plans because the road was flooded. A planter and his wife were powerfully converted, following which about a thousand souls were also converted, according to Shadford's personal experience. Shadford was a powerful, Pentecostal preacher and numerous eye-witness accounts of his work survive. Let's take two:

'It was quite common for sinners to be seized with a trembling and a shaking, and from that to fall down on the floor as if they were dead.'

'George Shadford strode to the front....."Who wants a saviour? The first that believes shall be justified." That did it; the place erupted... in a few minutes the house was ringing with the cries of broken-hearted sinners and the shouts of happy believers.'

A successful Primitive Methodist circuit centred on Scotter was led by men like George Rex of Retford and Hannah Parrott. The groundwork was done by Braithwaite who noted that 'the country was on a move for miles round, and many were converted to the Lord'. Thousands attended camp meetings at Hardwick Hill. A chapel was built in 1829, though the Primitive Methodists were tricked out of it and needed another one in 1849.

For a few days in 1829 Scotter became the venue for the group's national conference, at which it was decided to send missionaries to America. The revival of 1830 'was one of the most powerful and extensive...the country was baptised. Nearly every house was a house of prayer'. In 1839 Scotter sent J Scarborough as a missionary to the Channel Isles.

- *You can sit in the churchyard and copy Shadford's youthful practices.*

- *Visit Hardwick Hill, now rather lost within Laughton Woods in contrast to being covered with 'blown sand' in the nineteenth century.*

George Shadford: from Scotter to Virginia (Author's collection)

Scrooby:

A village of huge importance to American visitors because of its links with the Brewsters, Scrooby was also one of several places with a palace for the Archbishop of York from medieval times, most of which was demolished around 1558 and the rest around 1637, being replaced with a more appropriate farmhouse. Archbishop Thomas Wolsey stayed for some time in 1530 as he fell from grace, and is recorded as travelling to preach in various local churches. In 1536 noblemen gathered at the Palace as they responded to the rebellions.

William Brewster (senior) held the manor of Scrooby as bailiff to the Archbishop of York. Young William Brewster went to Cambridge in 1580 but stayed for barely a year. He returned to Scrooby and in 1590 replaced his father as bailiff, and then in 1594 became postmaster, a managerial role more related to maintaining the postal system on the Great North Road.

Scrooby was a 'chapel', not a parish church, and Brewster seems to have been able to bring Puritans to preach here, perhaps because it partly fell within the parish of Sutton where his brother held the living. Like the Wrays and the Denmans, Brewster did much good 'by procuring of good preachers'. The Puritan pastor Robert Southworth and Jane Wastneys were allowed to marry here in the early 1593 – with another Puritan, the curate Thomas Hancock officiating – and without the banns having been read legally.

The low-lying position of Scrooby adjacent to the Carrs is clear in this romantic old print. (Author's collection)

Not everyone was happy: in 1591, churchwarden William Throope complained 'one of his horses could preach as well as the curate', and Thomas Hancock, Scrooby's curate 1590-2, sued him.

In 1598, Brewster was in trouble for 'gadding' about to hear good preaching and 'publicly repeating' or discussing what he had learnt in afternoon sessions at the church - presumably from Richard Clyfton at Babworth. Brewster, the Jacksons and others were effectively acting as a church 'house group' might today. The churchwardens at Scrooby were not Puritan - they reported the latest curate, Henry Jones, for not wearing a surplice in 1598. Brewster's response to the charges showed that he was systematically using the curates to fill the gaps at Scrooby and Bawtry.

After Clyfton was removed from Babworth (and Henry Gray from Bawtry), some of his flock began listening to other preachers, such as John Robinson at Sturton in May 1605; Clyfton was cited in 1607 for 'pretending' to be curate at Scrooby (as was Southworth) and then Brewster's home was used for meetings - a small group lived in Scrooby in any case. Some of these decided on separation and emigration. Brewster resigned his position as postmaster in September 1607. He attempted to reach the Netherlands via Boston in 1607 but eventually arrived in 1608; some believe the women and children left Scrooby by small boat down the river. Orders to arrest Brewster and several other Scrooby people were issued in December 1607.

Having moved with Robinson from Amsterdam to Leiden, Brewster quickly became the leading elder. Brewster returned to England in 1619 and travelled on the Mayflower as the spiritual leader - though not ordained in any conventional sense. In New England he retained this spiritual role and

The remains of the old Manor House some 200 years ago in an old print. (Author's collection)

For a decade Brewster tried to run Scrooby church in line with his own views, but left in 1608. A local labourer seems intent on building his own version of the 'Mayflower', perhaps. (Author's collection)

was a studious and strong preacher until his death in 1644. Bradford wrote that he was:

> '… a man that had done and suffered much for the Lord Jesus and the Gospel's sake, and had bore his part in well and woe with this poor persecuted church above 36 years…'.

- *Visit the church, which certainly has many associations with rebellious Puritans from 1590 to 1608; next door is the 'old vicarage' where Brewster most likely called in!*

- *The remains of the Palace are across the road and in a field but there is little of real significance.*

Scunthorpe:

For some years this was the home of Salim Wilson (c1859-1946), a former Sudanese slave who was rescued by Charles Wilson of the Church Missionary Society and became a Christian in Nottingham in 1886, although he claimed some Christian influence from his childhood. After a small number of mission trips back to Africa, he became an evangelist with the Church of England, though later joined the Primitive Methodists in Scunthorpe, where he married his landlady. In 1988 relatives from Sudan visited his grave in Crosby Cemetery.

Skegby, nr Mansfield:

The 'Quaker House' here was the home of Elizabeth Hooton, the remarkable Quaker preacher and missionary, who became the first of Fox's followers in 1646-7. In 1647 Fox wrote: 'I met with a tender people, and a very tender woman whose name was Elizabeth Hooton...and with these I had some meetings and discourses'. Hooton had become disillusioned with the Baptists.

Signs and wonders were plentiful in Fox's ministry. Her son wrote: 'the mighty power of the Lord was manifest [and] startled [the members of] their former Separate meetings, and some came no more; but most that were convinced of the truth stood, of whom my mother was one and embraced it...'. The healing of a demon-possessed woman horrified those present by 'the stink that came out of her' as she writhed on the ground, but when she was healed she sat down calmly and said, "Ten Thousand praise the Lord."

Hooton was clearly a leader and in 1650 it was noted that 'from a true experience of the Lord's work in man, she felt herself moved publicly to speak the way of salvation to others'.

The first Quaker congregation was formed in this house and it became a Quaker meeting house; from 1673 to 1800 even burials took place here until it was sold to fund a new meeting house. It is not known at what time the Quaker burial ground there was first used or, for certain, that the house that became the Quaker meeting house was definitely Hooton's.

Elizabeth Hooton's house at Skegby, the tall one towards the left, is a remarkable survival at Skegby. (Picture the Past, Nottinghamshire County Council)

Many miraculous events are reported to have occurred; as Fox wrote, 'the Lord by his powers wrought many miracles to the astonishing of the world and confirming people of the truth...'. In 1654 Fox held a major meeting at Skegby, where 'the Lord's power went over them and all was quiet. The people were tuned to the Spirit of God, by which many came to receive his power'.

Hooton soon became a leading member of the Friends and their first woman minister, and was imprisoned in Derby as a result of 'reproving a minister' in 1651. Further spells of prison followed: York in 1652 following an offence in Rotherham, and Lincoln in 1654 (for interrupting services in the 'steeplehouse' at Beckingham, Lincs). and 1655. She became a frequent writer of letters of complaint and also a contributor to pamphlets. Her husband died in 1657.

In 1660 Jackson, the minister for Selston, violently assaulted her, allegedly without provocation, while she was walking along the road.

> 'On the 2d of the month called April (1660), Elizabeth Hooton, passing quietly on the Road, was met by one Jackson, Priest of Selston, who abused her, beat her with many Blows, knockt her down, and afterward put her into the Water.'

She is perhaps the earliest woman missionary we know of, making several journeys to New England and the West Indies. In 1661 she went to Boston with Joan Brocksopp of Little Normanton; she was immediately imprisoned in Boston, then she was abandoned in wolf-infested forests two days' travel out into the wilderness with just a few biscuits. She managed to return to Boston – via Rhode Island and Barbados! In 1662 she rented a farm in Leicestershire for her son, who was soon also arrested.

In London in 1662 Hooton followed Charles II around St James's Park, haranguing him and causing a scandal by refusing to kneel before him. Hooton was 'moved of the Lord and called by his Spirit to go to New England again'. She obtained a licence from the King to settle in any of the American colonies, but still found the Boston authorities resistant. She was stripped and whipped through three towns, before again being abandoned in the wilderness with 'many bears, wolves and deep waters'. She was left to walk through deep snow with a pregnant friend after her horse was seized by the King's Commissioners; she found her way by following the tracks of wolves. In March 1665 John Endicott, a governor of New England who had persecuted the Quakers, died; Hooton attended his funeral and, unsurprisingly, was arrested. Her testimony is one of the most explicit records of the oppression which had gripped New England, except Rhode Island, by the 1660s.

Hooton returned to England for most of the rest of her life, becoming a prominent author of letters and petitions. She was recorded as one of the 'heads and teachers' at Harby, Lincolnshire, in 1669. Her son Samuel took up the family tradition of going to New England and getting into trouble. He married at Skegby in 1670. In 1671 she joined Fox and others in a further trip to Barbados – her approach being evident from her letter to the island's rulers which began 'To the rulers and magistrates of this island that ought to rule for God'. There she died in 1672.

- *The 'Quaker House' at Skegby is a remarkable survival - a domestic house where we can identify Pentecostal life in the seventeenth century.*

Snarford:

Apart from being one of the most genuinely astonishing small country churches in England, Snarford is a treasure house of Puritan connections. Two generations of the St Paul family are splendidly celebrated here, but their friends and relations are just as significant.

The interest begins with George St Paul (1499-c.1559), who married Jane Askew, sister of the famous Protestant martyr of 1546, Anne, who was executed with John Lassells of Sturton and Gateford. George was a successful lawyer and close advisor to Charles Brandon, Duke of Suffolk, whose wife Katherine Willoughby (1591-80), was a leading evangelical at court and in Lincolnshire, and perhaps a great influence of the Queen, Catherine Parr. Edward Askew was in Cranmer's retinue. In the 1540s these people formed an influential network of Protestant reformers at Henry's court, which included John Lassells.

The St Pauls did well from the dissolution but both Anne Askew and John Lassells were burnt for heresy at Smithfield in 1546, in a crisis that nearly engulfed Willoughby and Parr.

Sir George St Paul was a leading puritan, but is his mother clutching a Prayer Book or a symbolic 'Book of Life'? Sir George would possibly have disapproved of the former more than the latter! (Janie Berry)

Sir George St Paul and his wife, Frances Wray, portray an image completely at odds with the term 'puritanical.' Lacking children, they devoted time and money to God's cause in Lincolnshire. (Janie Berry)

Sir George's will showed links by family and friendship to the Askews and also to Sir Christopher Wray – a significant connection for our story – but perhaps an ambivalent approach to the Reformation.

The central tomb is Sir Thomas St Pol. (St Paul) who died in 1582, and his wife. He was very active in Parliament. He is in armour, which is complete in every detail except for his helm, which lies under his head. This has on it an elephant with a castle. Both have a closed book in their hands, possibly representing a Prayer Book, but it also could be 'The Book of Life', which is now closed. He was a strong Protestant, firm in seeking out Catholic recusants.

The next tomb is of Sir George St Paul (1562-1613) and Frances Wray, married at the age of fifteen to Sir George in one of the most important marriages of the evangelical Protestants; after thirteen years she had the daughter Mattathia whose effigy lies in the alcove below her, but who died in 1597 before her second birthday, and was followed some sixteen years later by Sir George, a man once described by Lord Burghley as 'one of the best men in the country'.

Frances Wray appears rather set on going in a different direction to her husband, the Earl of Warwick. (Janie Berry)

Frances, her sister Isobel, and Katherine Willoughby were the leading evangelical women in the Midlands. George must surely have grown up to stories of his great aunt, burnt at Smithfield.

Sir George (1562-1613) had land throughout Lincolnshire including Melwood Grange and Snarford. He was also 'an ardent Puritan' and supported the same causes as Sir William Wray in Parliament.

His involvement with the Bill against 'scandalous clergy' in 1604 was 'to make fit the ground and to weed'.

After Guy Fawkes' failed plot, St Paul was on a committee to consider the Jesuits. In 1607 he was supporting the more free preaching of the Gospel, and in 1610 was supporting typically Puritan proposals to stop clergymen holding several benefices and to restrain 'excesses in apparel'.

St Paul condemned Catholicism as 'ambition, human policy and heathenish superstition'. He supported the Puritan clergyman Allen of Louth who was charged with not using the Prayer Book, and left him £5 in his will; Allen got a benefice at Ludborough through Wray influence, his daughter married a leading local Puritan cleric Thomas Rainbow, who was beneficed at a Wray stronghold in Blyton, and the Wrays sent his grandson, a future bishop, to university. This typifies how they worked.

Having no children, much of his wealth was spent on charity. He supported ten old men and women, and young tradesmen in Market Rasen, where he also funded a schoolmaster. At his funeral in 1613, he arranged an oration by Dr John Chadwick, the rector of Faldingworth. Chadwick referred to the 'six learned and profitable preachers … were brought up in the universities at his cost and charge'. His wife Frances and her sister Isabel arranged the Cambridge education of the Puritan rector of Worksop, Richard Bernard, and he credited his book, *Christian Advertisement*, to Sir George and Frances. In 1628, Bernard dedicated *Ruth's Recompense* to Frances Rich, as she had by then become.

On the wall is a memorial to Frances with her next husband Robert Rich, 1st Earl of Warwick, also a Puritan. Rich's previous wife was an adulteress but he chose not to divorce her so could not remarry until she died. In Essex, Rich supported evangelical priests just like the Wrays. Frances further endowed Magdalene and continued to support the university education of young Puritans such as Edward Reyner, who graduated in 1621. Frances made him the schoolmaster at the Market Rasen school, and he was a friend of John Cotton; Reyner was influential enough not to be too troubled by minor nonconformities, and became lecturer in Lincoln 1626 – a position which he held until Civil War broke out when he was nearly murdered in Lincoln Cathedral and preached at the Siege of Newark.

Frances was described in later life as 'a person of shining conversation and eminent bounty'. Rich and Frances were both buried at Felsted.

Her stepson, Robert Rich, who became the second earl, also had Puritan connections, which made him distance himself from Charles I and drew him to the New England colonies as well as Virginia. In 1628 he helped to get a patent for the Massachusetts Bay Company. He opposed Charles in the Civil War and commanded the Parliamentary navy, providing some help to the colony of Rhode Island in 1643. Richard Bernard's daughter, Mary, was married to Roger Williams, the founder of Rhode Island, so again we see that one small family proved to have connections across the globe.

How blessed we are to have these memorials still; in the 1840s Archdeacon Stonehouse wanted the tombs removed as 'dangerous', but there was an outcry.

- *This is a special place, visually stunning, but it also tells a story of commitment to the Gospel.*

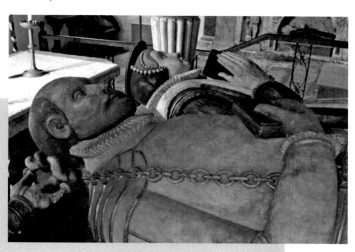

Sir Thomas St Pol. (St Paul) died in 1582; with an Askew as a mother, he must have grown up with stories about religious persecution. (Janie Berry)

Stow:

Legends claim that this ancient church owes its origins to Saint 'Etheldreda' (Æthelthryth, d.679), an East Anglian princess who first married in 652 despite a vow of perpetual virginity.

She retired to live as a nun on the Isle of Ely but in 660, for political reasons, was married off again to Ecgfrith, King of Northumbria. At first Ecgfrith also respected her vow but in 672 he changed his mind and attempted to take her from her nunnery. She escaped and made the long journey from Northumbria to Ely, crossing the Humber.

She avoided the Roman road for safety. Hot and weary, she prayed for a resting place and soon came across a pleasant flat meadow strewn with flowers, where she and her companions fell asleep:

> 'When, after a little while, she woke up from her sleep and rose to her feet, she found that her travelling staff, the end of which she had driven into the ground, dry and long-seasoned, was now clothed with green bark, and had sprouted and put forth leaves. Seeing this, she was stupefied with amazement and, along with her companions, she praised God and blessed him for this most extraordinary happening from her innermost heart.'

Saint Hugh is often depicted with his famous swan, as here in a window at Ordsall; it lived in the moat at Stow Park.

This place became known as 'Aedeldrethestowe' or 'Stow'; this was for long assumed to be Stow, but is now thought to be Stow Green near Threekingham in Kesteven. However, the image of Etheldreda planting her staff and it growing is a powerful emblem of the planting of the Gospel in people's hearts, and the planting of the Church.

In 870 the Danes are said to have destroyed Stow. Some say that a bishop was murdered here. Certainly the Danes wintered at Torksey in 873. By the tenth century Stow was one of several 'mother churches', and the Bishop of Dorchester rebuilt the church as a base for part of his diocese, although this church then burnt down. Stow Park became a manor of the bishops. Stow may have acted as the 'pro-cathedral' before Lincoln took over in 1072, when the see was translated there.

The church was rebuilt in the 1030s and extended in the 1070s; Earl Leofric of Mercia and his wife the famous Lady Godiva funded a college for secular canons at Stow between 1053 and 1055. Tales of Godiva's naked ride through Coventry did not emerge until the thirteenth century.

In 1186 the new Bishop of Lincoln, Hugh of Avalon, was warned that the manor pond had been invaded by a huge and vicious swan. The servants caught the beast and brought it to him, but instead of ordering it to be roasted he fed it on bread and it became his devoted friend – even cuddling up to him. The swan stayed at Stow when Hugh was away, but seemed to know when he was coming back by its excited flapping. When he slept it would guard him zealously and was known to nip the legs of annoying chaplains. After he died it remained on the pond, lonely, and is often shown beside him in illustrations.

In 1192-1200 one of the finishing touches on the northern pinnacle of the west front at Lincoln Cathedral was a statue of a swinesherd playing his pipes. The huge building project was always short of money as the people of the diocese laboured to match the project's needs, and Hugh was grateful for all he could receive. The story is that a young Stow swinesherd kept a few coins to give to the bishop who, mindful of Biblical principles about widows and mites, ordered the statue to be put up to show his gratitude.

In 1547 the manor of Stow surrendered to the King; although Stow retained an archdeacon (who did not live there necessarily) its role in the Church was diminished. In 1920 Archdeacon Wakeford was involved in allegations of adultery which, some argue, were engineered by his opponents within the Church; Wakeford had made many enemies over his abrupt handling of laxity amongst the clergy, including his own brother-in-law. The case did much to damage the Church, with the press finding the combination of Church and Sin an attractive theme.

In 1848 the vicar planned an extensive restoration of the building that would have been funded by the parish rates. This caused anger in the 'vestry' as its members thought 'a class of men calling themselves archaeologists have resolved to fasten upon the Church of Stowe and the parish funds, that they may use both for the display of their skill in the science of Antiquities'.

- *This ancient church is a good place to reflect on the longevity of the Christian Faith and how each generation has contributed to two thousand years of heritage. The pagan symbols on the font and the 'one tower inside another' seem to represent this. Take the window of Etheldreda as a symbol of the planting of God's Word in this landscape.*

- *Pause by the earliest known drawing of a Viking longship (tenth century) to consider the persecution of Christians that has occurred along the way, those who have suffered, and those who suffer still.*

Sturton-le-Steeple:

Sturton is of great importance in its connections with one martyr, two of the spiritual leaders of the congregations that moved to Netherlands in 1608, and at least one – if not two – of the Mayflower Pilgrims.

The Lassells family held land here and George, who had done work for Thomas Cromwell, acquired the manor in 1540 after Thomas Darcy was executed for his role in the Yorkshire Rising of 1536-7; George also owned Gateford near Worksop, knew the evangelical Hercy family and was the brother of the Protestant martyr, John (see Gateford). So the Lassells were aligned with the evangelical Protestants, whether by faith or vested interest.

John Smyth (c1570-1612) was the son of a Sturton man, about five years older than John Robinson. Whitley reported that he was 'a Sturton lad from the Habblesthorpe district of his uncle Thomas'. At Cambridge Smyth was influenced by Francis Johnson, at Christ's College, who later became an early 'Separatist' and formed a Puritan community in the Netherlands. Smyth became a Puritan 'lecturer' in Lincoln in 1600 but lost that position in 1602, living for a time as a physician but engaging in a lengthy legal battle which perhaps brought him into contact with Sir William Wray, an influential Lincolnshire Puritan to whom he dedicated his first book as 'my approved friend and benefactor'. He was cited for preaching without authority at West Burton in 1602. He was curate and schoolmaster at North or South Clifton, Notts, in 1603-4. During this time he became close to Thomas Helwys, a member of the local gentry with Puritan views.

This house is traditionally believed to be the home of John Robinson at Sturton, though it has been heavily altered since this picture was taken 100 years ago. (Picture the Past, Nottinghamshire County Council)

In 1604 Smyth was in trouble for preaching in Gainsborough, but it is likely he was living in South Clifton, where he was either – or both – curate and schoolmaster. In October 1604 a number of Puritans, including a John Smyth, were charged for illegal assembly over a riot – probably connected with the church at Marnham, across the river from Clifton. Another involved in this dispute was instituted to the living at Basford, close to Thomas Helwys's home, and where Smyth preached unlicensed in 1607. His unlicensed teaching in Gainsborough was defended by William Hickman and Sir Gervase Helwys. Around the time of the significant Puritan conference in Coventry, probably in 1605, he began to decide on separation and he became 'pastor' of a Gainsborough congregation after about January 1607, becoming one of the first to formally separate from the Church of England. He was criticised for being 'made minister by tradesmen'. Possibly Smyth went to the Netherlands before his congregation in 1607; the passage of both the Gainsborough and Scrooby groups appears to have been financed by Smyth's friend, Thomas Helwys. He did not leave behind fond memories of his homeland: 'infinite sorts of sinners … adulterers. Theeves, Murtherers, Witches, Conjurers, Atheists, Swaggerers, Drunkards, Blasphemers'.

Smyth is most important as a Baptist. In 1609 he re-baptised himself and then Thomas Helwys, forming the first English Baptist congregation. He later endured a bitter split with Helwys, although his final writings, before his death

The roadsign for Sturton fittingly combines a Roman and a Pilgrim. (Janie Berry)

in 1612, show a man who wished to heal old wounds. Bradford concluded he was 'a man of able gifts and a good preacher', but underestimated his long-term impact.

John Robinson (1576/6-1625) was educated at Gainsborough before going to Cambridge in 1592, then the centre of religious radicalism; three of its graduates were executed in 1593 for challenging the Church of England. Robinson was elected to a fellowship in 1597. He married Bridget White, also of Sturton, whose family had moved to Beauvale at Greasley where they wed in 1604. Jane White (later Thickens), Catherine, Roger White and their sister Frances, who married Francis Jessop at Worksop, all went to the Netherlands.

A connection with the Mayflower passenger William White has not been proved.

After a brief clerical career in Norwich, Robinson was disappointed in James I's policy in 1604 and was one of the Puritan clergy who were suspended. He preached at Sturton in May 1605; many attended from other parishes and seventeen local figures were in trouble for non-attendance at their own churches. The significance of this is that it came just two months after Clyfton had been deprived of his place at Babworth. By 1606 Robinson had become a 'Separatist' and was linked with Clyfton, eventually joining the Scrooby group after leaving Norwich probably in 1607. Like Clyfton, he began 'preaching about' and became, as Bradford later said, 'famous and worthy'.

In 1609 Robinson formed a congregation in Leiden, leaving Clyfton behind in Amsterdam, and with William Brewster as its senior elder. It was a small proportion of this congregation that left Leiden in 1620 under John Carver's leadership to travel to America. Carver was married to Catherine White, but his own origins are uncertain. That he married a Sturton woman and was clearly trusted to lead suggests a long association. We do not know if he was from Sturton (or indeed anywhere else) as no parish registers for Sturton have survived. However, the certificate of musters for the '30th year of Henry VIII' in Sturton lists a John Corver and a Richard Carver – along with George Lassells, several Smyths, a Legett and Thomas Whyt. Six years later a list of those who contributed 'benevolence' to their King includes a John Carver.

Catherine Carver was the daughter of Alexander White of Wybornedale in Sturton and most likely the sister of Bridget Robinson (nee White). She married her second husband, John Carver (c1565-1621), at Leiden by 1609 and he was nominated as the first governor of the new colony. Carver may have been living in Leiden before the English Puritans arrived. Although Carver played an active role in leading the Mayflower voyage, both he and his wife died within a few months of arriving in New England.

- *This is an essential place to visit although the evidence that 'Crossways' is really Robinson's house is very speculative.*

- *Habblesthorpe is now an overgrown churchyard; you can go here and speculate that Smyth may have come from this remote spot.*

Sutton cum Lound:

This was one of the 'Puritan' parishes that surrounded Retford, and James Brewster, the brother of William, held the living from 1594 until 1614, although briefly excommunicated in 1597. Several people were in trouble for non-attendance at church in 1598 and again in 1603, including Richard Clyfton's brother John and several who later went to Leiden. James Brewster was embroiled in a lengthy legal battle over Bawtry Hospital. In 1605 Edmund Thurland refused to take communion and was denounced by Brewster as a 'whoremaster', for which he was sued.

In 1608 Richard Clyfton illegally took some of the services here after being ejected from Babworth. A Nottinghamshire couple, Henry 'Cullandt' of 'Nottinghamshire' and Margaret 'Grymsdiche' of Sutton cum Lound were married in Amsterdam on 5 July 1608, having previously had their banns read by Clyfton at Sutton. It is also thought that the children Robert and Ann Peck, who went to live with Brewster at Leiden, were from this village and also a Margery Dale, recorded with the Amsterdam congregation.

In 1614 James Brewster was succeeded by another Puritan, Ezekiel Burton, who continued the tradition of non-compliance with Church expectations. While he was at Sutton a son, Hezekiah, was born in 1632. He also became a clergyman, and was admitted to one of the Wray fellowships at Magdalene, where he met Samuel Pepys. He became interested in psychic research but died, relatively early, in 1681.

Swinefleet:

This village is actually in Yorkshire, but it was almost home for John Wesley. It was another of the outlying places where Wesley preached sporadically as it was a convenient river port for him, but Swinefleet grew to have its own Methodist Society quite quickly – perhaps because it had long been neglected by the Church of England. The first time he preached, in 1766, there was heavy rain, which he expected to put people off, but the marshlanders gathered outside of the house to listen to him as best they could. Within a few years they had their own meeting house, but it was not big enough for when the great man visited so he preached 'on a smooth, green place, sheltered from the wind'. He preached a simple sermon and noted that many rejoiced to learn of 'being saved to the uttermost'. In 1788 he noted that the church was filled from end to end.

William Dealtry (1775-1847) grew up in Swinefleet and became a notable defender of missionary activity in India and a leading evangelical.

Tickhill:

Richard Jackson, one of the Scrooby congregation at the time of William Brewster, had moved to Tickhill by 1608. Tickhill was the home of Richard Farnworth (c1630-66) who, at the age of sixteen, had experienced his own conversion and began a journey of rejection of infant baptism, a belief in attaining spiritual perfection in this life, the rejection of formal worship, and constant prayer. George Fox's arrival at Balby in 1651 had attracted Farnworth's attention and, barely into his twenties, he became a preacher of Quakerism.

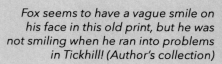

Fox seems to have a vague smile on his face in this old print, but he was not smiling when he ran into problems in Tickhill! (Author's collection)

He became an advocate of the laying on of hands to heal the sick, which he reputedly did in 1651, later writing about this in *Antichrist's Man of War* (1655). Indeed, Farnworth was one of the most important early Quaker writers and evangelists. He seems to have been a man of strong moods; one commentator said 'the sword of his mouth is very sharp', while another depicted him as a fat red dragon filled with fury!

Tickhill and nearby Balby became key Quaker bases. At Tickhill in 1652 Fox noted a 'mighty brokenness' amongst the people in his meeting, but then went to the parish church. There the clerk hit him with the Bible, so that his face bled. He was thrown over a hedge and dragged through the street. Fox got back to the meeting of his Friends, where the Tickhill priest soon arrived with his own supporters and denounced them as 'Quakers'. But when Fox began to preach, the priest began to shake and someone called out, "Look how the priest trembles and shakes, he is turned a Quaker also."

Treswell:

This seems to have been one of the Puritan churches around Retford but the picture is confused because there were two 'medieties' until 1764. Around 1607-8 Puritans like John Robinson and Edwards of Marnham preached here; Robinson also preached at neighbouring South Leverton. In 1610 many parishioners were fined for refusing to attend services with their new rector. Henry Langley, here from 1611-36, was involved in a famous 'possession' case at Mansfield and published a book on the Lord's Prayer in 1616; he was a correspondent of John Cotton, the famous Boston Puritan. Langley had been at Christ's College and then a curate in Axholme previously. Unsurprisingly, he was in trouble in 1635 for having no altar rail.

Treswell had Langley for one mediety, but had an absentee, Mr Lincoln, in another. His work was done by Edwards, who was clearly a Puritan too as he did not wear a surplice.

John Viccars (1604-60), the son of a freeholder at Treswell, went via Cambridge to be vicar of St Mary's Stamford in 1627. However, he was too progressive for some parishioners, who denounced him for heresy. Viccars had divided his parishioners into the godly and the ungodly, holding prayer meetings and fasts that attracted visitors. Bishop Williams cautioned him, but the parishioners, including some innkeepers, took their case to Laud's High Commission. Viccars had some controversial opinions, especially on sex; he thought that 'if a man Knowe his wife after her conception with Childe, or when shee is past Childe bearing, it is both murther [murder] and adulterie'. It was also adultery for a man to sleep with his wife three days before or after taking the sacrament. He condemned other priests who did not preach twice on a Sunday to 'the fire in hell'. He thought that the 'common prayers' were not enough for salvation and attacked individuals in his sermons. He also had his devotees and the women among them refused to work for 'ungodly' masters and were castigated as 'the newe nunnery of Stamford'.

For his supporters Viccars organised a fast and preached some sermons up to six hours long before he went to London. Several locals appeared in his defence at the High Commission in 1631, saying his accusers were drunkards and reprobates. However, the Bishop of St David's accused Viccars of having turned 'the pulpit into a place to vent his malice upon the poor people of Stamford'. One historian called him 'an arrogant prig'. He was defrocked, fined and imprisoned, but recanted after a few years and had six years in ministry in Essex before further troubles. He was a noted linguist and travelled extensively, but his submission to Laud's pressures undermined his authority.

Viccars' sister Helen married William Sampson of South Leverton, who became a poet and dramatist. They had two sons (see Clayworth) and after William's death Helen married Obadiah Grew, supposedly on the deathbed recommendation of her first husband. Grew lost his Coventry benefice at the Restoration and became a celebrated nonconformist; this was a marriage of leading Puritans!

In 1661 the priest was Thomas Rainbow, who had severe doubts about the new prayer book but was 'vehemently urged to conform' by his wife. Perhaps suspecting Rainbow would refuse, the parish clerk brought a copy of the book to him - according to the version told by Calamy. Rainbow then managed to be ill on Sunday so that he did not have a problem reading - or not reading - any passages, but then he became so ill in reality that Death beckoned him. His last words to his wife were, supposedly, "If thou couldest have trusted God, thou mightiest have had a living husband, and a livelihood for thyself and children; but now art like to lose both." There are several things about this story that don't quite fit into the chronology (such as the date of his death compared to the arrival of the Prayer Book) but there remains an intriguing possibility that this might be a relative of Edward Rainbow who became Bishop of Carlisle.

Twigmoor:

This isolated place between Scunthorpe and Brigg was a centre of Catholicism during Elizabeth I's and James I's reigns. The manor belonged to the Tyrwhitts; in 1580 the young Lord Sheffield was living in Sir Robert Tyrwhitt's house at Kettleby, when his tutor became alarmed that his sons were converting

Sheffield to Catholicism and resorting to 'the Church of Twigmore' for masses with Robert Tyrwhitt.

Five of them were arrested and imprisoned; it is likely at least one died in prison and Sir Robert died in 1581.

In 1597 Anthony Atkinson wrote to Sir Robert Cecil for permission to use armed ships from Hull to root out the recusants. 'This place is one of the worst in Her Majesty's dominions and is used like a Popish college for traitors' one of Cecil's agents wrote, who pointed out that 'great woods, caves and vaults' aided the Catholic agents.

Fugitive priests said Mass there in 1604. John, or Jack, Wright lived here and became involved in Catesby's 'Gunpowder Plot' of 1605, because of which he moved his family away. He had been involved in a plot in 1601 and was said to be one of the best swordsmen in the land. Also involved were Ambrose Rookwood, married to one of the Tyrwhitt daughters, and her cousin Robert Keyes; these were both executed in 1606. Jack Wright was killed in fighting in Worcestershire, although his brother escaped.

The site was riddled with underground hides and in 1940 a complete underground stable was discovered.

Wheatley, North and South:

The two villages at Wheatley had two churches, but that at the South village has long since fallen into decay. (Author)

Hugh Bromhead, believed to have been curate at North Wheatley around 1605, is little known, but he and his wife became Separatists in about September 1607 - possibly after he had been 'deprived.' It is likely that he was related to Thomas Brumhedde, vicar of Rampton, who was removed under Mary I for being married and thus was most likely an evangelical. He penned a remarkable denunciation of the Established Church:

'Babylon, the mother of all abominations, the habitation of devils, and the hold of all foul spirits, and a cage of every unclean and hateful bird'.

Bromhead went with his wife Anne to the Netherlands and stayed a member of John Smyth's congregation there until they asked to join the Waterlanders' Church in 1609/10. He sent a letter from the Netherlands to a cousin in autumn 1608, which described the services in Helwys's church: four hours long, with much reading from the Bible and prophesying upon it. Clyfton says that Bromhead and Edward Southworth from Smyth's congregation tried to persuade him to renounce infant baptism.

Worksop

Worksop Priory was founded as an Augustinian priory in about 1103 by William de Lovetot; Norman nobles founded many monasteries so that their souls could be prayed for.

The de Lovetots married into the de Furnivals and Gerard made his name as a knight under King John and became a crusader, dying in Palestine in 1219. His body was brought back for burial in Normandy. Two of his sons also went to Palestine and Thomas de Furnival died in battle there in 1228. His younger brother, also Gerard, had Thomas buried and then returned home. Their mother, Maud, was very distressed about Thomas being buried in a heathen land and, it seems, sent her younger son straight back to the Holy Land. Thomas - or at least his heart -- was dug up and eventually buried on the north side of the Priory church wearing a helmet 'richly adorned with gems'. A tomb was erected, described as 'a noble carbuncle'.

'Crusader crosses' can be seen either side of the south doorway to the Priory, which are said to have been cut by the Furnival family as votive marks. John of Tickhill, Prior from 1303, commissioned an illustrated psalter; this contains four hundred and eighty two illustrations of the story of David and Solomon. It disappeared at the dissolution and in the eighteenth century turned up in the library of the Marquess of Lothian. Sadly, it is now far from home - it was bought by the New York Public Library in 1932.

In 1533-4 two men of Dutch origin were arrested in Worksop for holding Lutheran views, characterised as 'Lollard.' Although both appear to have repented, their views were quite extreme for the time: denying the 'real presence', tithes, and most of the 'powers' of priests. Their case shows that reforming books were in circulation, and they were clearly active in the area.

The Priory was dissolved on the orders of Henry VIII in 1539. The manor was granted to Francis Talbot, fifth Earl of Shrewsbury, on condition that the Earl provide a glove for the right hand of the sovereign at the coronation. This tradition continues to this day. The gatehouse became the vicarage and, from 1628, a school.

In the Priory is a memorial to one of the Lassells (Lascelles) family. The full story of the martyr John is told under Gateford.

The important Puritan clergyman, Richard Bernard (c1568-1642), from Epworth, went to Cambridge funded by the Puritan Wrays and then became vicar of Worksop in 1601 under the patronage of the Puritan Whalleys. He knew all the key local Puritans, including Helwys and Smyth. He was deprived of his living in 1605, for nonconformity, and associated with members of

The old priory gatehouse at Worksop served later as a vicarage and then a school. (Author)

Smyth's congregation at Gainsborough. During 1606-7 Bernard had his own large covenanted congregation at Worksop, gathering people from other parishes yet still within the Church of England, which some suggested was to stop people deserting to Smyth at Gainsborough, but later, in 1607, under the influence of the Archbishop Matthew and the Puritan Arthur Hildersham, Bernard recommitted to the Church of England and his 'living' at Worksop. He became an opponent of the Separatists, with works such as *Christian Advertisements and Counsels of Peace* (1608), which angered Smyth, who called him a 'chameleon' who 'pretended zeal for the truth and faith of Christ'. Smyth accused him of having coveted the livings of 'Sawenby' and Gainsborough, saying Bernard wrote a pamphlet urging against bishops, 'but there was weakness in his character, and when it was proposed to print it, he dared not fix his name'.

Bernard remained staunchly Puritan; he refused to use the sign of the cross in baptism at Worksop and, after moving to Somerset in 1613, got into trouble for refusing to genuflect and for departing from the set prayers. However, Bernard is also an interesting writer of many Christian books including *The Faithfull Shepherd* and *The Isle of Man*, an influence on John Bunyan. He was interested in the supernatural, claiming to have exorcised a demon whilst at Worksop.

The combination of ancient and modern makes Worksop Priory an extraordinary building. (Author)

In 1627 he published *A Guide to Grand Jury Men*, which denied that a 'good' witch could exist and argued for the execution of all who had signed up with the Devil.

Bernard may not have crossed the Atlantic, but his influence did. His fourth son, Masakiell, sailed to New England with the Puritan preacher, Joseph Hull; his daughter Mary emigrated in 1631 with her husband Roger Williams. They would become the founders of Providence, Rhode Island, and the first Baptist church in America; they also took with them views on religious tolerance that derived from the writings of Smyth and Helwys.

Several people with Worksop connections went to the Netherlands with the Pilgrims. There John Murton, a key member of Smyth's Gainsborough congregation, married Jane Hodgkin of Worksop in 1608; Murton became the second leader of the Baptist Church in England and a notable writer on religious liberty.

Richard Bernard of Worksop was a great puritan preacher and author, but he experienced a turbulent relationship with Smyth and Helwys.

The Hodgkins family went to Amsterdam; Rosamond Horsfield also came from Worksop as did William Jepson, both moving on to Leiden with the Robinson group.

It is also possible – though unproven – that the boy William Button, baptised here in 1605, was the one who died on the Mayflower voyage.

After Bernard left in 1613, the authorities tried to bring in a non-Puritan vicar over the Puritan curate James Collie, who was already installed in the vicarage, the old monastery gatehouse. When the benefice was awarded to Oliver Bray, Collie clung on, not letting his successor into the vicarage. Collie called Bray a 'dumb dogge' and said children baptised by him were damned. When Bray suddenly died in 1615 a local woman was accused of poisoning him and put on trial in Retford, but records of the result have been lost.

However, during the nineteenth century the aristocratic patrons managed to eradicate all traces of 'enthusiam' in their choice of vicars.

John Wesley only once preached at Worksop and, having perhaps read his Journal for 1780, its people might have preferred if he had never visited at all:

> 'I was desired to preach at Worksop; but when I came they had not fixed on any place. At length they chose a lamentable one, full of dirt and dust, but without the least shelter from the scorching sun. This few could bear, so we had only a small company of as stupid a people as I ever saw.'

Chad Varah (see Barton) was educated at Worksop College. Curiously, the town has never had a Baptist church, though it has one of the few long-running Congregational churches.

- *See the crosses etched in the doorway of the Priory, the Lassells memorial and the old gatehouse, but also walk round behind the Priory to understand what an extraordinary conglomerate building it is.*

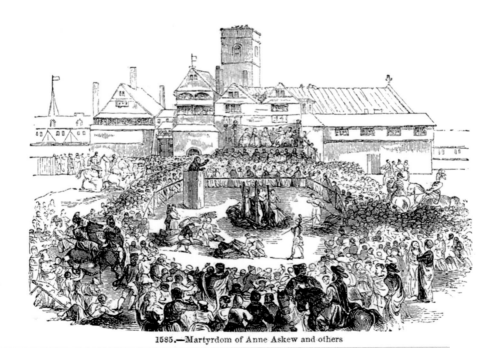

1585.—Martyrdom of Anne Askew and others

In this version of the Askew-Lassells martyrdom, Anne appears to be seated off to the left from the others. (Author's collection)

Wroot:

John Wesley was briefly curate here although the church he used has been replaced; apparently he used to go swimming in the dykes. A small village with little income for its parson, it was never an attractive posting. It was derided in verse by Wesley's sister, Mehetabel:

'Fortune has fixed thee in a place
Debarred of wisdom, wit, and grace –
High births and virtue equally they scorn,
As asses dull, on dunghills born…'

John Wesley's brief period as a curate has a sombre sign giving no indication that he liked to go swimming! (Author)

137

When Samuel Wesley held the living as Rector he complained that it barely brought in £50 a year, of which he paid Mr Whitelamb, the curate, £30. In 1733 he asked that the living be transferred to Whitelamb, who was a local boy 'took from among the scholars of a charity school', who then assisted Samuel on his study of Job.

Whitelamb's illustrations in Wesley's Job book were condemned by one critic as 'amongst the worst that ever saw under the sun'. At this time the master of Wroot Charity School was John Romley, the curate who so memorably banned John from the pulpit, but who identified Whitelamb's potential. Samuel Wesley then helped Whitelamb to go to Oxford in 1731, though he was too poor to own a gown, then to be ordained and hold a curacy. The curate married the rector's daughter, Mary, and Samuel noted that 'they love the place, though I cannot get anyone else to reside upon it.' Whitelamb was made rector but Mary soon died.

Whitelamb was one of those listening when John first preached on his father's tomb. John Wesley and Whitelamb later fell out over doctrine; Stonehouse, the historian of Axholme, thought he had become a 'deist'.

That a school existed at all here was due to the will of a Mr Travis, who in 1706 left money to found free schools in Thorne and Wroot specifically for the 'poorest children'.

- *A marker stone by the cemetery gates to note John Wesley's curacy, 1727-9, and there are memorials to Mary and John Whitelamb. By the gate is a faded village sign depicting Wesley.*

- *Visit the 'Wroot Travis Charity School' to reflect on how Christian charity sought to meet the needs of the poor.*

INDEX OF PERSONS